SPEAKING OF SPEECH
New Edition

Basic Presentation Skills for Beginners

Student Book

David Harrington
&
Charles LeBeau

MACMILLAN

About this Book

Welcome to the new edition of *Speaking of Speech*! The first edition was a bestseller for more than a dozen years. We have kept what you liked and improved the rest.

Organization of the New Edition

The popular, step-by-step approach of the first edition remains basically the same. The new edition still divides the complex, communicative activity of speech into The Three Messages. We still start with the simpler, less abstract, less language-dependent skills of the Physical Message (posture, eye contact, gestures, and voice inflection), thereby allowing the students to make quick, visible progress and gain confidence. However, in response to your feedback, the new edition reverses the order of the Story Message and the Visual Message, giving visuals greater emphasis. After all, we say "show and tell," not "tell and show."

Regarding the structure of each unit, we still divide each unit into four sections that systematically explain **what** the target skill is, **why** it is important, **how** to use the target skill, and give activities to **practice** the target skill. In the new edition, the **what** and **why** sections are simplified so that more time can now be spent in class on the interactive **how** and **practice** sections.

New: The *Speaking of Speech* DVD

Over the years, teachers have asked again and again if we knew of any sample speeches for students to watch and emulate. We couldn't find any examples that were suited to the level, needs, and interests of our students, so we decided to make our own *Speaking of Speech* DVD. The eight sample speeches on the DVD correspond with the Performance sections in the student text.

Each episode is short and sweet with an average running time of about three minutes, and was filmed in front of an audience of eager listeners. The sample speech itself is bracketed at the beginning and the end with commentary by the Emcee, played by the talented Jimmy Wolk. At the start, he sets the stage for each speech and, at the end, he focuses our attention on the *Speaking of Speech* target skill. The Emcee's physical skills, his posture, eye contact, facial expressions, and gestures make him a great model for students to emulate! The speeches on the DVD also exemplify different types of visuals including photos, posters, and graphs. For low-level learners, a closed caption option allows viewing with subtitles.

New: Expanded and Updated Visual Message

Over the last few years, computer presentation software has become ubiquitous. This has been both a blessing and a curse. Although this software provides the user with endless choices of color, font, clipart, layout, and templates, there have also been reports of student presenters preparing an infinity of word charts, and then boring their classmates and teachers to death by tediously reading the sentences on the charts. (Even more disturbing are reports that a few teachers have retaliated in kind in their own presentations!)

The new edition has addressed this problem by expanding the section on visuals. Episode 4 of the DVD features what we hope is a humorous delivery of a bad set of slides, followed by an improved presentation of better slides. Episode 5 features the same slide delivered twice, first in a long, redundant explanation, then, redone with a short, systematic explanation. Additionally, we asked our gifted illustrator, Ty Semaka, to catalog a list of "Dos and Don'ts" for presenting slides.

A final note. In *Speaking of Speech*, we have tried to create a world of possibility, a world of things not as they are, but how they could be. We don't know the answers for a better tomorrow. But we do know how they will be reached: through improved communication, especially through improved presentation skills. Join us. Help us.

Be part of the solution!

David Harrington
Charles LeBeau

Table of Contents

The Physical Message (pp. 7–38)

Unit	Speech Skill	Performance	DVD
1 (pp. 9–17)	Posture and Eye Contact —the foundation of the Physical Message	Learners perform an informative speech of their hometown or a city they recommend visiting.	In Episode 1, Lisa Suzuki recommends visiting her hometown, Portland, Oregon.
2 (pp. 18–27)	Gestures —support your words with the Physical Message	Learners prepare and perform a speech describing the layout of a convenience store, an amusement park, or a school campus.	In Episode 2, Josh Carlin takes the audience shopping at his neighborhood convenience store.
3 (pp. 28–38)	Voice Inflection —emphasize key words to help the audience remember	Learners prepare and present a speech demonstrating how to prepare or cook a dish of their choice.	In Episode 3, Terri Lou teaches the audience how to make her favorite snack.

The Visual Message (pp. 39–56)

Unit	Speech Skill	Performance	DVD
4 (pp. 40–50)	Effective Visuals —create visuals that speak to the audience	Learners choose two countries and prepare comparison charts of the two countries.	Episode 4 contrasts the visuals of two presentations on a new hybrid car.
5 (pp. 51–56)	Explaining Visuals —explanations that get the most out of your visuals	Learners perform their country comparison speeches after preparing explanations for their visuals.	Episode 5 contrasts two explanations of the same slide.

The Story Message (pp. 57–95)

Unit	Speech Skill	Performance	DVD
6 (pp. 62–68)	The Introduction —engaging the audience from the start	Learners prepare and present the introduction to a product comparison speech.	Episode 6 features three speakers presenting on the same topic to different audiences.
7 (pp. 69–86)	The Body —using evidence and transitions to build your message	Learners prepare and present the body to their product comparison speech.	In Episode 7, Justin Martin presents the body of his product comparison speech.
8 (pp. 87–95)	The Conclusion —a simple formula for summarizing your presentation	Learners prepare and present the conclusion to their product comparison speech.	Episode 8 features three conclusions on the same topic to different audiences.

Final Performance (pp. 96–99)

Evaluation Forms (pp. 100–108)

The Three Messages in a Speech

The Physical Message

Not all communication in a speech comes from words. The way you stand, where you look, how you use your hands and vary your voice send a message as well. In this book, we call that the Physical Message.

The Visual Message

Speech is not just about what you say. What you show and how you show it is as important as what you say. In this book, we call that the Visual Message.

The Story Message

A speech is like a story. It has a beginning, a middle, and an end, all connected together into a single message. Keeping the parts in order, and connecting them together is called the Story Message in this book.

The Physical Message

What Is the Physical Message?

Just as words form the spoken language, how we stand, where we look, how we move our hands, and the tone of our voice form the body language. This Physical Message includes four skill areas.

- **Posture:**
  The way we stand and position our whole body.

- **Eye Contact:**
  Where we look to keep in touch with the audience as we speak.

- **Gestures:**
  How we move our hands to support our words.

- **Voice Inflection:**
  The way we change the tone of our voice to emphasize key words.

Why Is the Physical Message Important?

A good Physical Message sends a confident, positive, energetic and enthusiastic message to the audience.

Practice: Physical Message Pairwork

Take turns trying to communicate the following words or phrases to your partner.
You may choose randomly from A to U. Don't say anything to your partner. Use only body language.

 **Students A & B**

Step 1 Act out the words.
Step 2 Guess the words.
Step 3 Check the box next to the correct guess. 

- **A** I don't understand.
- **B** No.
- **C** Come here.
- **D** Speak louder, please.
- **E** It's down the street on the right.
- **F** Go!
- **G** Could I borrow your eraser?
- **H** Could I use your pencil?
- **I** Please sit over there.
- **J** What are you talking about?
- **K** You go first.
- **L** Look over there.
- **M** Don't stand there.
- **N** I have a question.
- **O** I'm hungry.
- **P** Give me all of your money.
- **Q** Please have a seat.
- **R** Follow me.
- **S** You're late!
- **T** Stop!
- **U** Who . . . me?

Speaking of Speech New Edition

Posture and Eye Contact

What Are Posture and Eye Contact?

The way you stand (posture) and where you look (eye contact) communicate a message. This is not a spoken message, but a *physical* message. Good posture and eye contact send a confident, positive message to the audience.

- **Posture:**
  The foundation of the Physical Message.

- **Eye Contact:**
  Gives you feedback from your audience.

Are they interested?

Do they understand?

Why Are Posture and Eye Contact Important?

Posture is the foundation of the Physical Message. If your posture is solid, you look confident. If your posture is weak, you look nervous and unsure.

Good eye contact gives you valuable feedback from the audience: Do they understand your speech? Are they enjoying your speech?

Posture: How Not to Do It

Look at these common posture and eye contact problems. Listen and match the problems with the descriptive labels in the Word Box, and write your choices in the spaces provided. The first one is done for you.

Word Box

- the pendulum   • the surfer   • the Leaning Tower of Pisa
- the hula dancer   • the birdwatcher   • the stargazer
- washing your hands   • the soldier

---

1. Swaying from side to side is poor speech posture because it communicates that you are also swaying back and forth between ideas in your mind.

    ● We call this "___the pendulum___."

2. Leaning to one side is poor speech posture because it is too relaxed, and makes the audience feel that you aren't serious about your speech.

    ● We call this "_____."

3. Looking up at the ceiling while giving a speech is poor eye contact because it shows that you aren't well prepared and don't know what to say.

    ● We call this "_____."

4. Moving your shoulders and upper body around as you speak is poor speech posture. It makes the audience feel that you are not calm, and not confident about your message.

    ● We call this "_____."

5. Swinging your hips back and forth and from side to side is poor speech posture because it shows that you are nervous, and not comfortable with your message.

   ● We call this "_____."

6. Rubbing your hands together as if you were washing them or playing with something in your hands is poor speech posture because it shows that you are nervous.

   ● We call this "_____."

7. Looking out of the window or staring at the back of the room is poor eye contact for a speech because it makes the audience feel that you are not interested in them.

   ● We call this "_____."

8. Standing stiffly at attention with your feet together and your hands at your sides is poor speech posture because it makes you look nervous and uncomfortable in your role as speaker.

   ● We call this "_____."

Posture: How to Do It

Making a good first impression is important. Even before you say your first word, your posture and eye contact should show the audience that you are calm, well-prepared, confident and ready. If you begin with good posture and good eye contact, it will be easy for you to maintain a positive Physical Message throughout your speech.

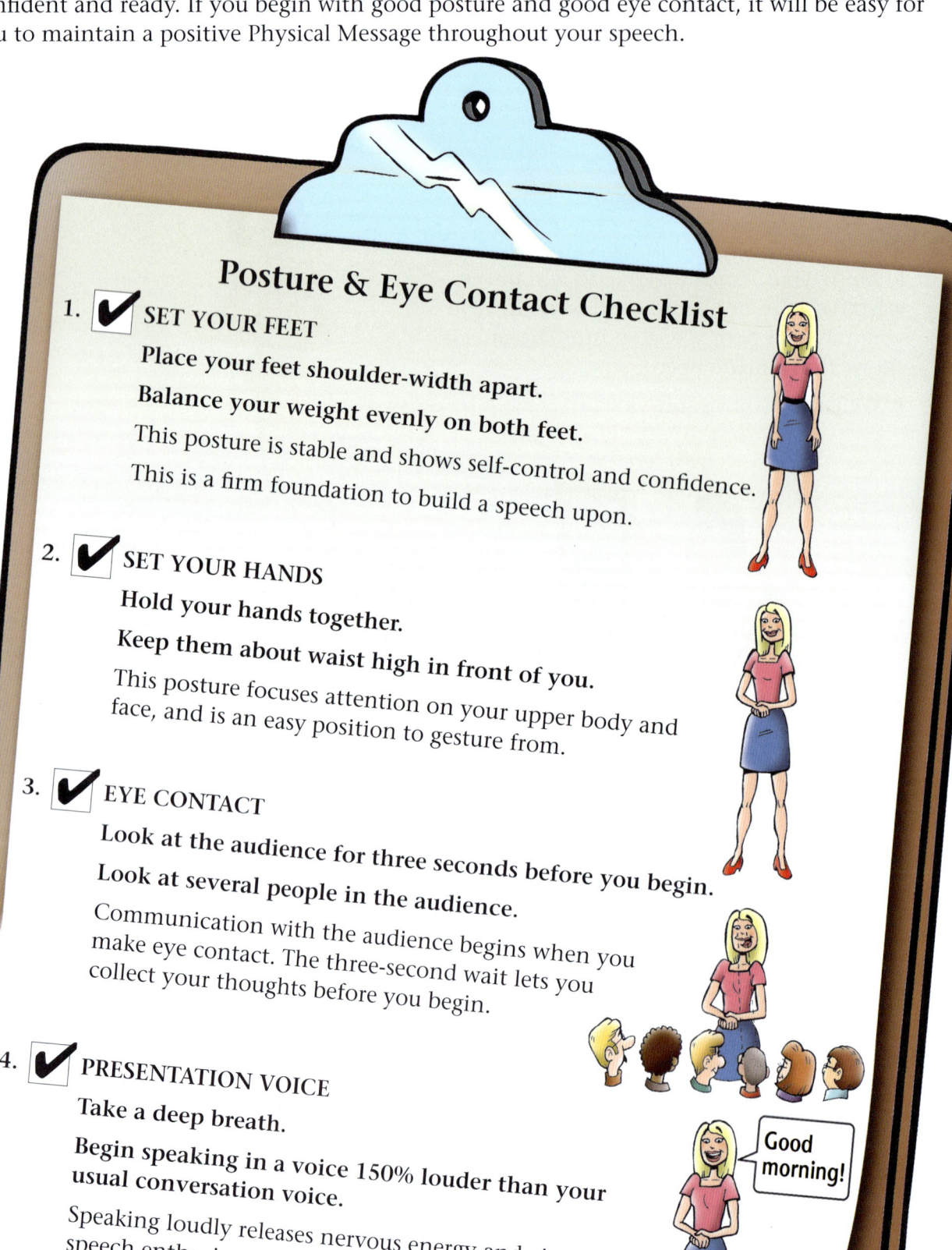

Posture & Eye Contact Checklist

1. ✔ **SET YOUR FEET**
   - Place your feet shoulder-width apart.
   - Balance your weight evenly on both feet.
   - This posture is stable and shows self-control and confidence.
   - This is a firm foundation to build a speech upon.

2. ✔ **SET YOUR HANDS**
   - Hold your hands together.
   - Keep them about waist high in front of you.
   - This posture focuses attention on your upper body and face, and is an easy position to gesture from.

3. ✔ **EYE CONTACT**
   - Look at the audience for three seconds before you begin.
   - Look at several people in the audience.
   - Communication with the audience begins when you make eye contact. The three-second wait lets you collect your thoughts before you begin.

4. ✔ **PRESENTATION VOICE**
   - Take a deep breath.
   - Begin speaking in a voice 150% louder than your usual conversation voice.
   - Speaking loudly releases nervous energy and gives your speech enthusiasm.

Speaking of Speech New Edition

Practice: Posture Workshop

Step 1 Group Practice

Stand up as a class and follow the Posture & Eye Contact Checklist:

- ✔ SET YOUR FEET
- ✔ SET YOUR HANDS
- ✔ EYE CONTACT
- ✔ PRESENTATION VOICE

Step 2 Individual Practice

Work in groups. Form a line. One by one, walk to the front of the group and practice getting set for a speech. Follow the Posture & Eye Contact Checklist and say "Good morning" or "Good afternoon" in your presentation voice.

Step 3 Repeat the individual practice, and this time say:

"Good morning. My name is _____."

The Physical Message 13

Practice: Posture and Eye Contact Workshop

Speaker:
Work in groups. One by one, come to the front of the group to practice communicating with the audience through eye contact. First, set your feet and hands, then carefully control your eye contact by looking at each person. Start with the person on the left. Look into their eyes for three seconds. Count out loud "1, 2, 3." Move your eyes to the next person to the right, make eye contact, and count "4, 5, 6." Continue until you have made eye contact with everyone.

Audience:
Raise your hand when the speaker makes good eye contact with you. Keep your hand raised as long as the speaker keeps eye contact. As soon as the speaker looks away, lower your hand.
- Lower your hand if the speaker doesn't have good eye contact, looks over your head, looks at the ceiling, or looks anyplace but in your eyes.
- There should only be one hand in the air at any time.

PERFORMANCE

Informative Speech

SPEECH TYPE:

In Episode 1 of the *Speaking of Speech* DVD, Lisa gives an informative speech on her favorite city. Giving an informative speech is like teaching. If you are giving an informative speech, your job is to teach something to the audience. The success of your speech depends on whether the audience learns what you wanted to teach.

SPEECH SKILL:

In an informative speech, eye contact is especially important. By watching the audience's faces, you can know whether they understand the information. If the people in the audience are nodding in agreement, it's a good sign that they understand what you are trying to teach. On the other hand, if people look puzzled, that's a sign that you need to try explaining the idea again.

SPEECH PREPARATION:

For this speech, you will use a quadrant, like the one Lisa uses, to help you prepare a presentation on the city you recommend visiting.

PERFORMANCE

Model: Informative Speech

FIRST VIEWING:

Watch Episode 1 of the DVD. Close your textbooks and enjoy the speech! After viewing, answer these questions:

1. What is the topic of her informative speech?
2. How many points does she have?

SECOND VIEWING:

Watch again and complete the evaluation form below. Fill in the activities for "SEE," "DO," "EAT" and "GETTING AROUND."

Informative Speech Evaluation Form

Speaker's name: _Lisa Suzuki_

City: _____

SEE	DO
EAT	GETTING AROUND

Did the speaker use the Posture & Eye Contact Checklist? ✓ Yes ☐ No

Did the speaker look at you? ✓ Yes ☐ No

Speaking of Speech New Edition

Speech Preparation

Assignment: Prepare an informative speech telling your classmates about your hometown or a city you recommend visiting.

PLAN:
Use a quadrant to brainstorm.

SEE	DO
• Portland Art Museum • (NBA Basketball) • Oregon Museum of Science and Industry • (Red Hot Chili Peppers)	• Shopping — (Nordstrom) — Saturday Market — Lloyd Center — (Niketown) — Powell's Bookstore
EAT	GETTING AROUND
• Old Town Pizza • Saigon Kitchen • (Jake's Famous Crawfish Restaurant)	• Car • Bus • (Bicycle) • MAX train

PREPARE:
Make a poster. Use photographs or draw pictures yourself.

PRACTICE:
Concentrate on your posture and eye contact.

PERFORM:
Speakers, use your visual to explain. Listeners, fill in the evaluation form on page 100.

The Physical Message

Gestures

What Are Gestures?

Gestures form the vocabulary of body language. This physical vocabulary supports the words of your verbal message. Gestures can be divided into four groups.

● **Number/Sequence**
These gestures signal a sequence, a process, or a number worth remembering.

● **Emphasis/Focus**
These gestures signal a key word, or an idea that you want the audience to focus on.

● **Illustration/Location**
These gestures help the audience visualize size, shape, and dimension, or help the audience visualize how to do something.

● **Comparison/Contrast**
These gestures help the audience understand similarities, differences, and changes.

Why Do We Need Gestures?

Gestures energize your presentation. They animate your presentation. They punctuate your presentation with meaning. Gestures signal that you are numbering, sequencing, emphasizing, demonstrating, illustrating, or comparing information.

How to Use Gestures

Just as there is a vocabulary for spoken language, there is a vocabulary for body language. The spoken language and the body language combine to help the audience understand your message. Here is a glossary of gestures for you to practice. Stand up and practice saying the words and doing the gestures together in class.

Glossary of Gestures

● **Number/Sequence**

Gestures for Number/Sequence help the audience visualize numbers or understand a process from beginning to end.

"I have **three reasons** . . ."

"The **first step** . . . the **second step** . . . and the **third step** . . ."

"Moving from **phase one** . . . to **phase two** . . . to **phase three** . . ."

● **Emphasis/Focus**

Gestures for Emphasis/Focus make your speech interesting and help the audience understand which words are important.

"Our product is **unique** . . ."

"The point I want to **emphasize** is . . ."

"The key point is **here** . . .!"

The Physical Message

● Illustration/Location

Gestures for Illustration/Location help the audience visualize the size, the shape, the location, the dimension, the action and many other aspects of your explanation.

"My TV screen is **this big**!"

"It is shaped **like this**."

"It is located in the **top right corner**."

"Twist it **like this**."

"It's in the **middle**."

"Pull it apart **like this**."

"It is on the **left**."

"The new notebook computer is **very thin**."

"Cut it **twice**."

20 *Speaking of Speech New Edition*

● Comparison/Contrast

Gestures for Comparison/Contrast help the audience understand differences, advantages, and changes.

"Both sides should be **equal** . . ."

"The price of gas is **higher now** than last year."

"**On the one hand** there's price, and **on the other hand** there's quality."

"World population has been rapidly **increasing** since the 1970s."

"**In the case of** China, . . . , and **in the case** of Brazil, . . ."

"These are **different**."

- Gestures not only help the audience understand; they add excitement and energy to your speech.
- A variety of gestures gets the audience's attention and keeps them interested in your message.

The Physical Message

Practice: Using Gestures

Step 1 Help Honest George make his speech more interesting by choosing the best gesture for each TV screen. Write the letter of the gesture on the TV screen. The first one is done for you.

"Hi! I'm Honest George. There are **three** [B] good reasons to vote for me.

First, [___] I have **more** [___] experience than anyone else in government. **Second**, [___] I have a **powerful** [___] program to **increase** [___] business. **Most important**, [___] you should vote for me because I will **cut** [___] taxes by **5%** [___]. Thank you."

A  — B  — C  — D  — E

F  — G  — H  — I

Step 2 Now that you have matched the gestures to the words, listen to the CD. Then stand up and read the speech out loud using the gestures shown.

Speaking of Speech New Edition

1. Small
2. Big
3. Round
4. Square
5. Triangle
6. Long
7. Short
8. Tall
9. Low
10. Three points
11. First
12. Fat
13. Thin
14. Equal
15. Better than

Practice: Gesture Pairwork

 **Student A** *(Student B: Please turn to the next page.)*

Step 1 Read the words above to your partner. Your partner should repeat the words and add gestures.

Step 2 Listen to your partner. Repeat the sentences and add gestures.

The Physical Message

Practice: Gesture Pairwork

Student B

Step 1 Listen to your partner. Repeat the words and add gestures.
Step 2 Read the sentences above to your partner. Your partner should repeat the sentences and add gestures.

1. There are two problems.
2. Global warming is a big problem.
3. A ring is round.
4. We want to cut costs.
5. New York is larger than London.
6. It's a big book.
7. Open the laptop.
8. Open the laptop and insert the DVD.
9. My room is small.
10. My room is small and has a low ceiling.
11. I want to talk about a growing problem.
12. First, I want to talk about a growing problem.
13. This is the point I want to emphasize!
14. Use a wide variety of gestures.
15. First, input your password, then hit "Return."

PERFORMANCE

Layout Speech

SPEECH TYPE:

In Episode 2 of the *Speaking of Speech* DVD, Josh Carlin gives a layout speech about his neighborhood convenience store. A layout speech tells the audience where things are, their size, and their shape. When you give a good layout speech, the audience feel confident that they can get around and find what they want. If your speech is unsuccessful, the audience will have trouble finding what they are looking for and might even get lost.

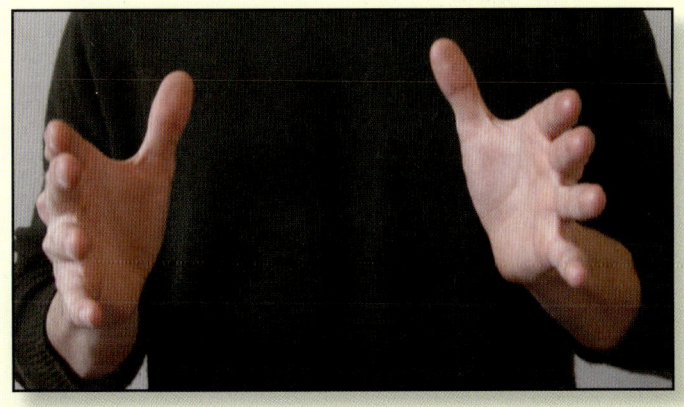

SPEECH SKILL:

Gestures are essential to a layout speech. Showing with gestures is better than just telling with words. It's much easier to *show* where something is than to *tell* where something is. And, from the audience's point of view, it's much easier to visualize where things are if you use gestures.

SPEECH PREPARATION:

For this speech you will use a grid, similar to the one that Josh uses, to help you plan and present your layout speech.

The Physical Message 25

PERFORMANCE

Model: Layout Speech

FIRST VIEWING:

Watch Episode 2 of the DVD. Close your textbooks and enjoy the speech! After viewing, answer these questions:

1. How many sections does he divide the store into?
2. How many points does he have?

SECOND VIEWING:

Watch again and complete the evaluation form below. Fill in the grid with items from the store. The first one is done for you.

Layout Speech Evaluation Form

Speaker's name: _____

Place: _____

		Potato chips Taco chips

Did the speaker use gestures? ✓ Yes ☐ No

Speaking of Speech New Edition

Speech Preparation

Assignment: Prepare a layout speech about, for example a convenience store, amusement park, or your school.

 **Step 1** PLAN:
Choose a kind of grid to explain your ideas.

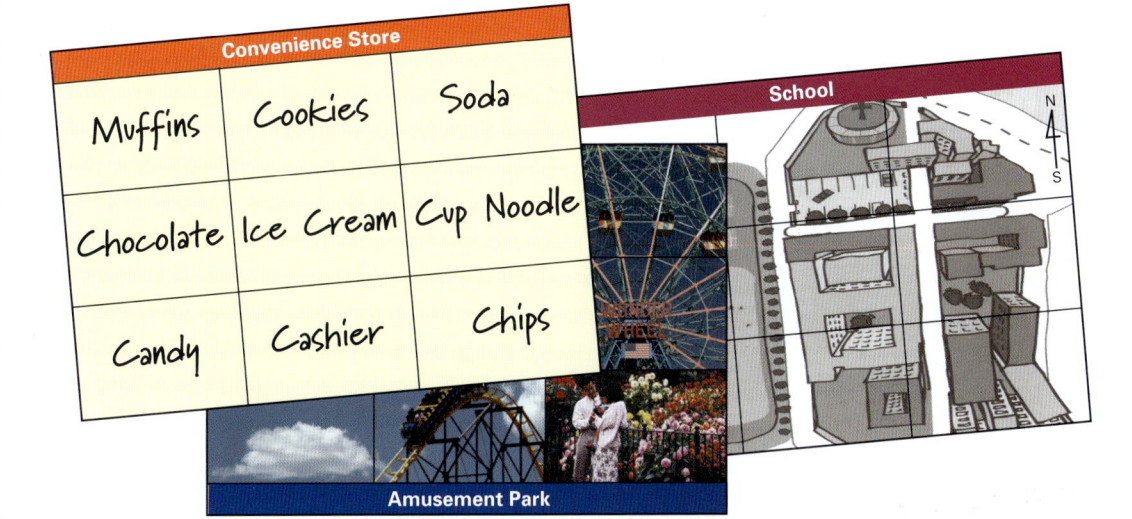

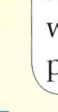 **Step 2** PREPARE:
Make your visual. You can use words, such as the convenience store words above. You can use pictures, such as the amusement park picture. Or you can use a map, such as the school map.

 **Step 3** PRACTICE:
Concentrate on your gestures.

 Step 4 PERFORM:
Speakers, use your visual to explain. Listeners, use the evaluation form on page 101.

The Physical Message

Voice Inflection

What Is Voice Inflection?

Voice inflection means changing your voice. You can change your voice in one of three ways. Listen to these three examples.

1. Stressing a word or phrase

I have a **LOT** of experience.

2. Stretching a word or phrase

No . . . I have a **Lo⟷t** of experience.

3. Pausing before a word or phrase

No . . . I have a ( ) . . . **LOT** of experience.

Why Is Voice Inflection Important?

Using inflection is a lot like using gestures. Without gestures your physical message is flat—there is no variation, no action, no energy. Similarly, without inflection your verbal message is flat—there is no variation, no color, no emphasis. Inflection emphasizes key words to add interest and help the listener understand your speech—just as gestures do.

Listen to the two radio advertisements. Which announcer uses voice inflection?

☐ Advertisement 1   ☐ Advertisement 2

How to Identify Voice Inflection

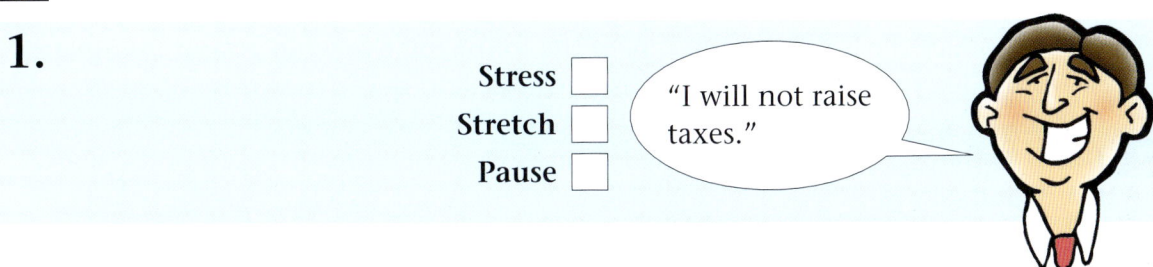

We've just heard an example demonstrating stressing, stretching, and pausing. Now, listen to these sentences and check the type of inflection that is used.

1. Stress ☐ Stretch ☐ Pause ☐ — "I will not raise taxes."

2.  "Climate change is a real danger!" — Stress ☐ Stretch ☐ Pause ☐

3. Stress ☐ Stretch ☐ Pause ☐ — "It's been a long time."

4.  "There are more than 400 different birds in the jungle." — Stress ☐ Stretch ☐ Pause ☐

5. Stress ☐ Stretch ☐ Pause ☐ — "It's bigger, better, and more exciting."

6.  "There is no down payment." — Stress ☐ Stretch ☐ Pause ☐

The Physical Message

How to Use Voice Inflection

- In the previous exercise you listened to the CD and were able to identify three types of voice inflection. Now it is time for you to decide for yourself which words to emphasize by stressing, stretching, or pausing.
- Which are the best words to inflect?
- Usually the inflected words are from one of the following five word groups: numbers, action words, descriptive words, comparison words, and negative words.

Step 1 Listen to the CD and underline the inflected word or words for each of the five word groups.

Numbers

"This is a $19,999 car."

"The universe is only 6,000 years old?"

"The universe is billions and billions of years old."

1.   ⋀ Stressing

2.   ⟷ Stretching

3.   ( ) Pausing

Action words

"We have cut prices in half."

"We can decrease pollution."

"The price of gas has shot up again."

4.   ⋀ Stressing

5.   ⟷ Stretching

6.   ( ) Pausing

Descriptive words (adjectives and adverbs)

"Do you still drive a big car?"

7. _____

∧ Stressing

"Attitudes are slowly changing."

8. _____

⟷ Stretching

"You can quickly increase your income."

9. _____

( ) Pausing

Comparison words

"We build more efficient cars than before."

10. _____

∧ Stressing

"We have the most experienced teachers."

11. _____

⟷ Stretching

"Nobody gives better service than us."

12. _____

( ) Pausing

Negative words

"And remember, there's no down payment."

13. _____

∧ Stressing

"Sorry, tax is not included."

14. _____

⟷ Stretching

"You should never drink and drive."

15. _____

( ) Pausing

Step 2 Now, listen again and repeat after each sentence. Emphasize the inflected words that you underlined.

The Physical Message

Practice: Inflection Pairwork

 **Student A** (Student B: Please turn to pages 34 and 35.)

China has the world's largest population.

China has the world's LARGEST population!

Step 1 Read the following 10 sentences one at a time to your partner. Your partner should repeat the sentence and add voice inflection and gestures.

1.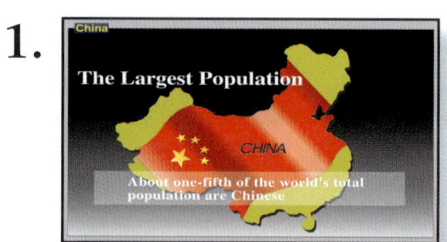
   - China has the world's largest population.
   - About one-fifth of the world's population is Chinese.

2.
   - There are over one billion people in China.
   - That's more than double the population of all the countries in the E.U.

3.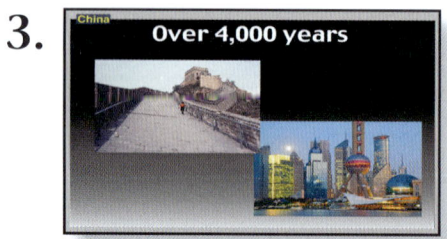
   - China has a very long history.
   - It is over 4,000 years old.

4.
   - Its history is divided into many periods.
   - The first period was the Xia dynasty in the 20th century BC.

5.
   - It was the first country to use gunpowder.
   - The Chinese invented fireworks.

32 *Speaking of Speech New Edition*

Step 2 Look at the slides below. Your partner will read two sentences for each slide. Listen to the sentences your partner reads. Repeat the sentences and add voice inflection and gestures.

1.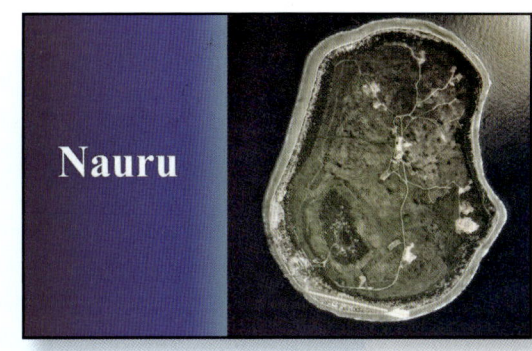

2.

3.

4.

5.

Practice: Inflection Pairwork

 Student **B**

 China has the world's largest population.

China has the world's LARGEST population!

Step 1 Look at the slides below. Your partner will read two sentences for each slide. Listen to the sentences your partner reads. Repeat the sentences and add voice inflection and gestures.

1.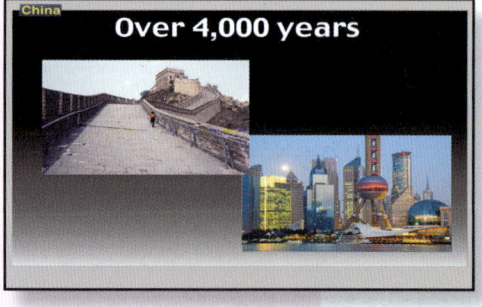

2. Over 1,000,000,000 people in China

3. Over 4,000 years

4. Xia Dynasty, Yin Dynasty, Sui Dynasty, Tang Dynasty, Song Dynasty, Yuan Dynasty, Ming Dynasty, Qin Dynasty, Qing Dynasty, Han Dynasty, Republic of China, People's Republic of China
   30 25 20 15 10 5 B.C./A.D 5 10 15 20 Century

5.

Step 2 Read the following 10 sentences one at a time to your partner. Your partner should repeat the sentence and add voice inflection and gestures.

1.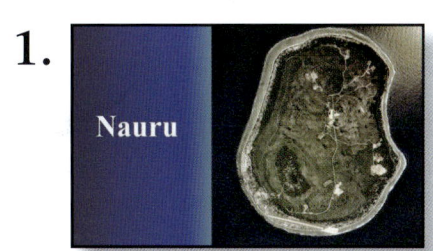
   - Nauru is one of the world's smallest countries.
   - It is only 21 square kilometers in size.

2.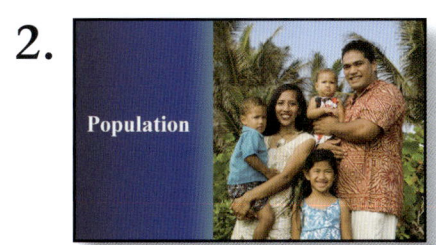
   - There are fewer than 15,000 people in Nauru.
   - Ninety percent of the people are unemployed.

3.
   - The first people arrived in Nauru 3,000 years ago.
   - Traditionally there are 12 clans or tribes.

4.
   - Nauru was administered by Australia, Britain, and New Zealand until 1968.
   - It declared independence on January 31st 1968.

5.
   - Nauru's economy was based on the mining of phosphates.
   - It used to be one of the richest countries in the world, but now it is one of the poorest.

The Physical Message

PERFORMANCE

Demonstration Speech

SPEECH TYPE:

In Episode 3 of the *Speaking of Speech* DVD, Terri demonstrates how to make a tuna sandwich. A demonstration speech is a type of informative speech. But in a demonstration speech we aren't just trying to inform the audience—we are trying to teach them how to do something. If, at the end of your speech, the audience can perform the activity you demonstrated, your speech has been a success.

SPEECH SKILL:

All the elements of the Physical Message are essential to a good demonstration speech. You need good posture to show your confidence. You need good eye contact to confirm that the audience understands the steps you are demonstrating. You need good gestures to demonstrate each step clearly. Finally, you need good voice inflection to emphasize the key words the audience should remember at each step of the demonstration.

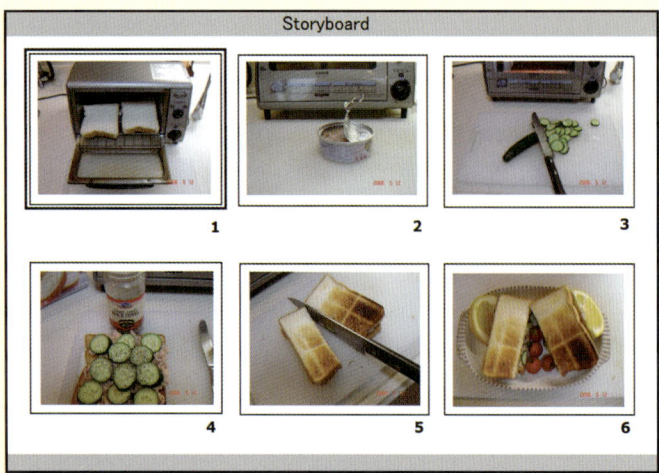

SPEECH PREPARATION:

For this speech, you will use a storyboard to help you prepare, and then use photos or drawings to illustrate each step.

Model: Demonstration Speech

FIRST VIEWING:

Watch Episode 3 of the DVD. Close your textbooks and enjoy the speech! After viewing, answer these questions:

1. What is she demonstrating?
2. How many steps are there?

SECOND VIEWING:

Watch again and complete the evaluation form below. Write the steps and the warnings. The first one is done for you.

Demonstration Speech Evaluation Form

Speaker's name: _Terri_

What did the speaker demonstrate? _____

Steps	Warnings
1. Toast the bread	Don't burn

Did the speaker use voice inflection? ✓ Yes ☐ No

The Physical Message   37

PERFORMANCE

Speech Preparation

Assignment: Prepare a demonstration speech on how to make a favorite dish.

Step 1 — **PLAN:**
Use a storyboard to break the process into easy "bite-size" steps.

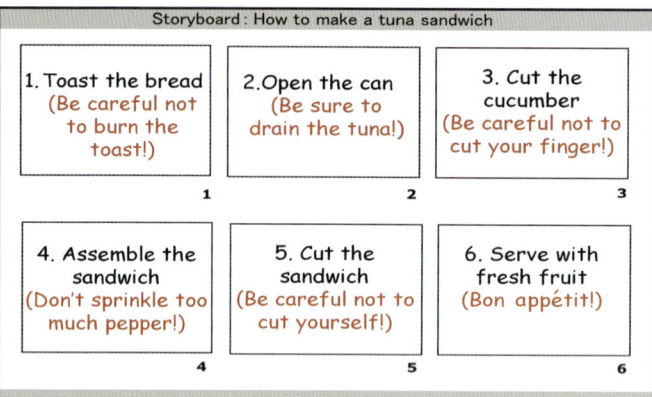

Step 2 — **PREPARE:**
Illustrate the steps using photos or drawings.

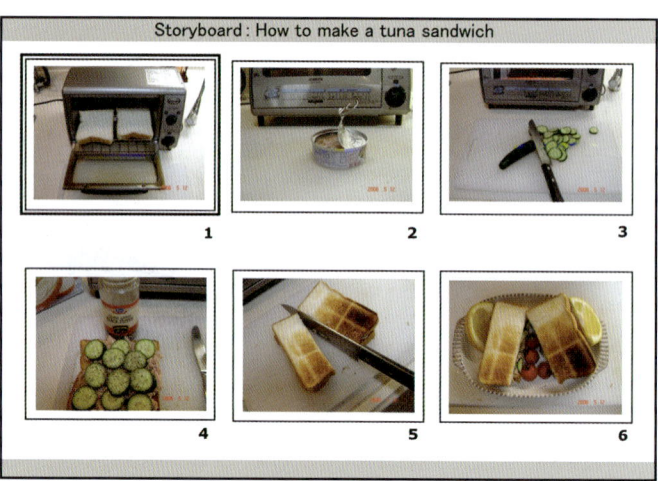

Step 3 — **PRACTICE:**
Be sure to practice all the physical skills, especially voice inflection!

Step 4 — **PERFORM:**
Speakers, use your visual to explain. Listeners, use the evaluation form on page 102.

The Visual Message

What Is the Visual Message?

One picture is worth a thousand words. Save time—use visuals! Show the audience with images; don't just tell them with words.

- **Effective Visuals:**
The images we show the audience.

- **Explaining Visuals:**
The words we use to guide the audience through the visuals.

Why Is the Visual Message Important?

The Visual Message is important because even if you stumble over sentences, mispronounce words, or get the numbers wrong, the audience will still understand.

Effective Visuals

FIRST VIEWING:

Watch Presentation 1 of Episode 4 of the DVD. Pay close attention to the slides the speaker uses. Close your textbooks and enjoy the speech!

1. How did he do?
2. Did you notice any problems with his visuals?

Slide Analysis

Analyze the following slides and write the problems and their possible solutions below.

1. **Green Machine Features**

    1. The best thing about the Green Machine is that it is economic to drive. The Green Machine's patented hybrid engine has an estimated combined city/highway 51.5 miles per gallon rating. In terms of percentage, this means that the Green Machine gets 18% more miles per gallon than the average new auto. This translates into a saving for the owner of 18% on gasoline. Ratings are based on estimated mileage for model year 2010. Note that for the 2010 models, the way that the estimated economy ratings were determined was revised.

    2. A second, related feature is that the patented hybrid engine generates less pollution. The Green Machine generates 70% less smog-forming emissions including CO_2 and other gases that have been proven to contribute to global warming. You can do your part in reducing global warming! Be part of the solution! Test drive a Green Machine today.

    3. In addition to emitting fewer dangerous gases and pollutants into our planet's atmosphere, the Green Machine contributes to reducing noise pollution, a particularly important factor in city driving. The Green Machine has been rated by *Driver and Car* magazine as being eight decibels quieter than the average new car. In the both the starting and driving phases, the Green Machine has been rated as quieter. This gives you, the driver, a safer, more comfortable driving experience.

    Problem

    Solution

2. **Green Machine Popularity**

MONTH	SALES
May	8,140
June	8,120
July	8,840
August	8,920
September	9,230
October	20,912
November	60,732
December	70,322

    Problem

    Solution

EFFECTIVE VISUALS

3.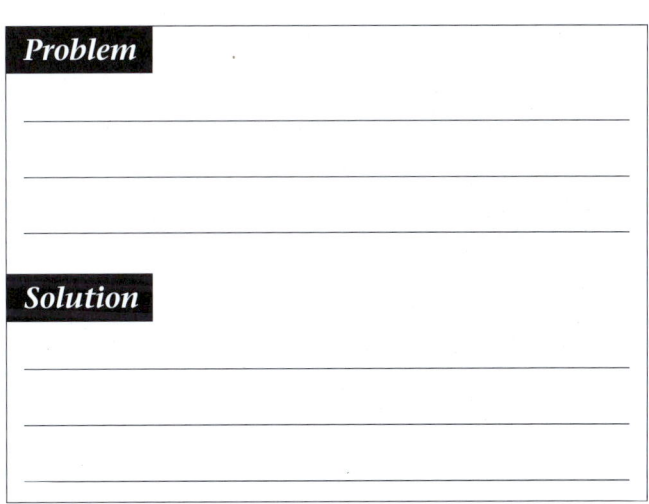

Problem

_____
_____
_____
_____

Solution

_____
_____
_____
_____
_____

4.

Conclusion

Remember:
If you care about the environment,
If you believe in recycling,
You'll love *Green Machine!*
(Green Machine is sold on a first-come, first-served basis. Performance is based on standard ratings and may vary depending on local driving and weather conditions.)

Thank you for your attention!

Problem

_____
_____
_____
_____

Solution

_____
_____
_____
_____
_____

The Visual Message

SECOND VIEWING:

Watch Presentation 2 of Episode 4 of the DVD. Note the changes in the visuals. Close your textbooks and enjoy the speech!

| Presentation 1 | Presentation 2 |

Compare your slide analysis to the solutions below.

Problem
- Speaker can't remember main points

Solution
- Use an overview chart

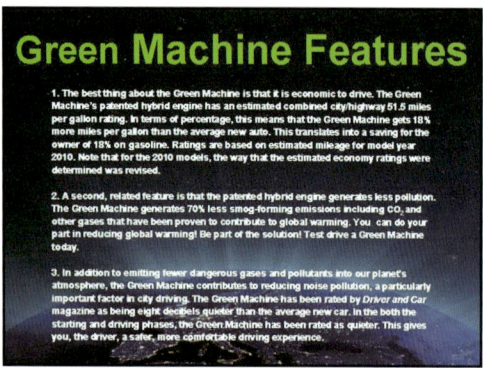

Problem
- Font point size is too small
- Long sentences
- Noisy background

Solution
- Use a large point size
- Avoid sentences
- Use a simple background

Speaking of Speech New Edition

Presentation 1

Problem
- Difficult to visualize a trend

Presentation 2

 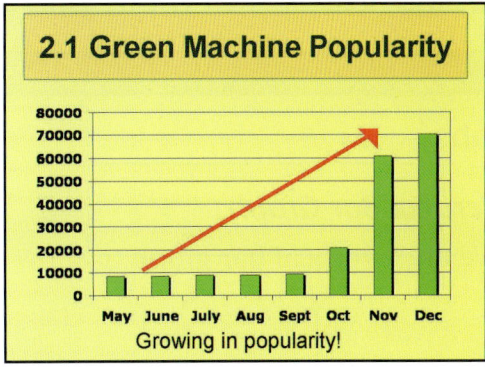

Solution
- Show ideas with images (graphs, illustrations, photos, etc.)

Problem
- Wrong kind of chart to show percentages

 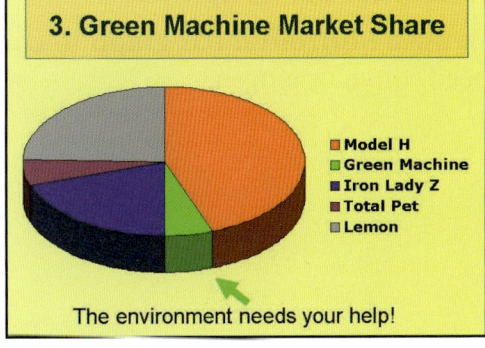

Solution
- Choose the right kind of chart to communicate your message

Problem
- "Noisy" conclusion chart
- Font is too small

Solution
- Use a simple conclusion chart like this one
- Make sure the font is large enough

EFFECTIVE VISUALS

The Visual Message 43

What Are Visuals?

Different ideas need different visuals. Look at the slides below.

Glossary of Visuals

- **Graphs**

    Vertical Bar Graph

    We use a **vertical bar graph** to show ranking.

    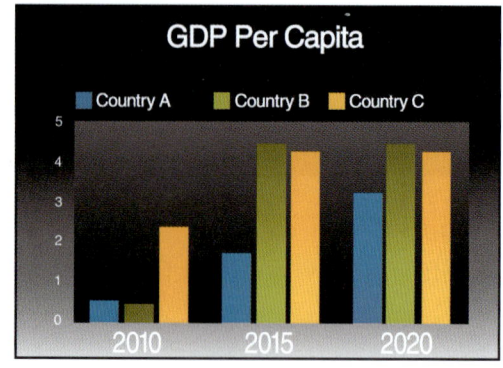

    Horizontal Bar Graph

    We use a **horizontal bar graph** to compare speed, time, or length.

    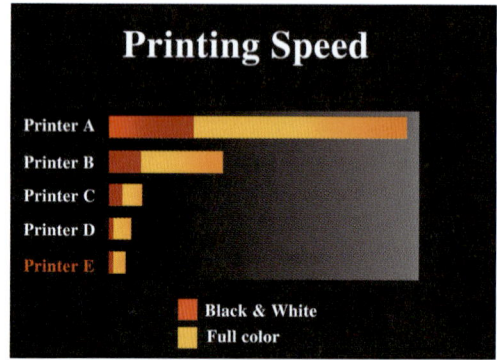

    Pie Graph

    We use a **pie graph** to compare percentages.

    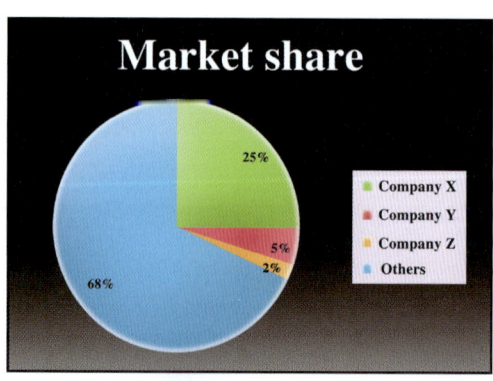

    Line Graph

    We use a **line graph** to show trends over time.

    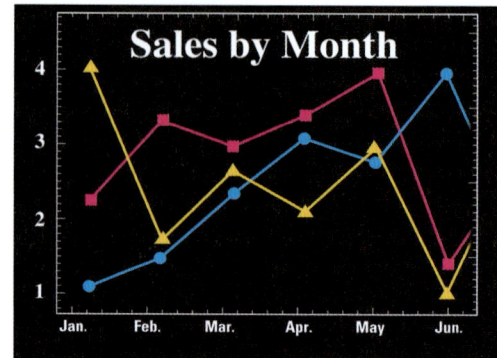

● **Pictures**

Photograph

We use a **photograph** for realism and to show details, or to create emotion.

Illustration

We use an **illustration** to emphasize only key points. We often use an illustration in place of a photograph for a simpler, clearer look.

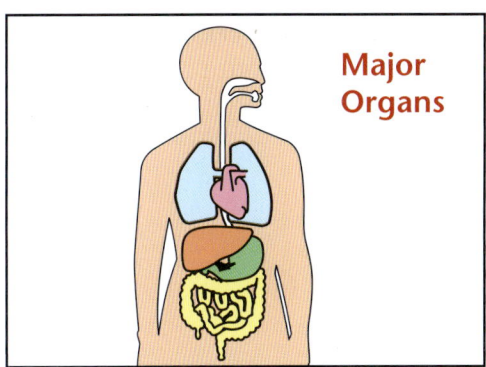

Map

We use a **map** to show layout and location. A floor plan of a building, such as a store or train station, is one kind of map.

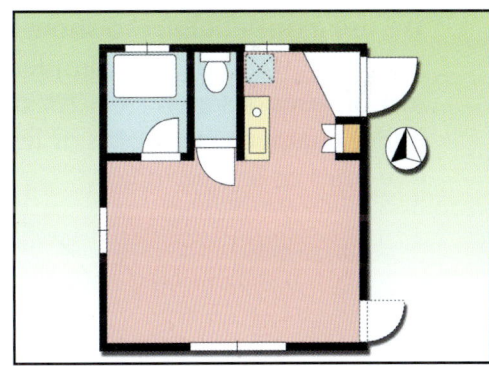

Diagram

We use a **diagram** to show the dimensions and features of an object. Diagrams are often used in technical presentations or product presentations to show the parts of an item.

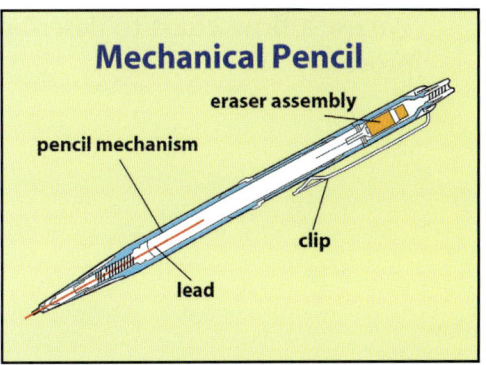

The Visual Message

● **Charts**

Title

We use a **title chart** to state the topic and its importance to the audience.

Overview

We use an **overview chart** to preview the contents of our presentation.

Bullet

We use a **bullet chart** to show lists of ideas. Note that we don't use complete sentences—just phrases or key words. Try to limit your bullet charts to five words or less per line and five lines or less per chart.

Flow

We use a **flow chart** to describe a step-by-step process.

How to Make Visuals: Guidelines

Guideline 1: Show Images

Show the audience your information by changing words and numbers into images.

- *Change a confusing table of numbers into a graph.*

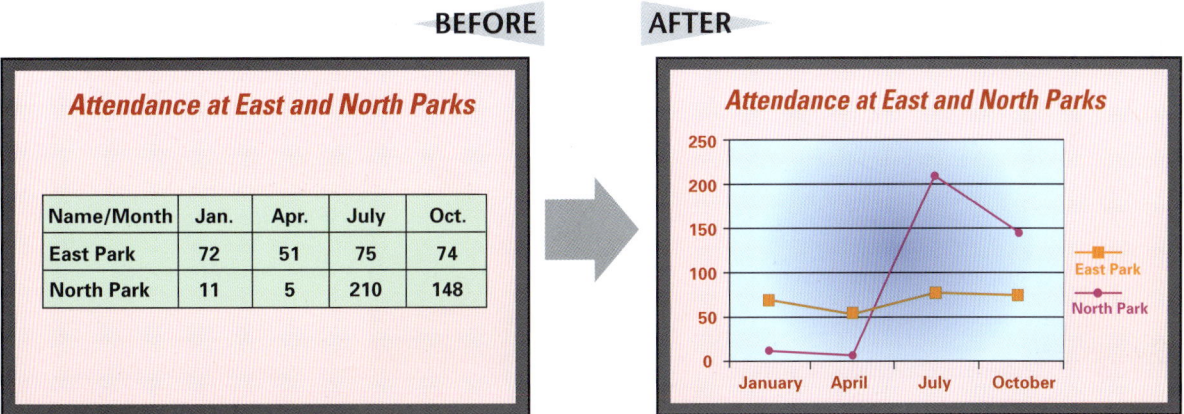

- *Change a list of locations into a map.*

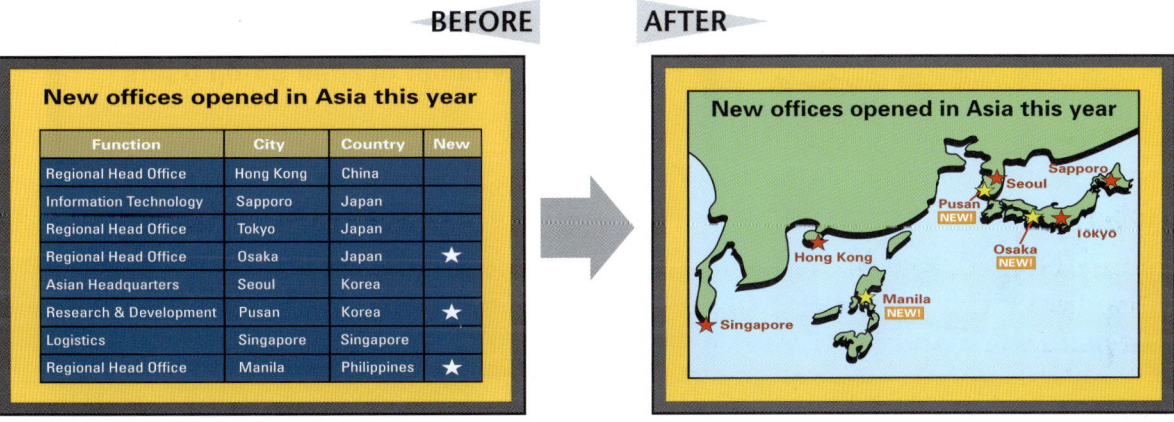

- *Change words into a flow chart.*

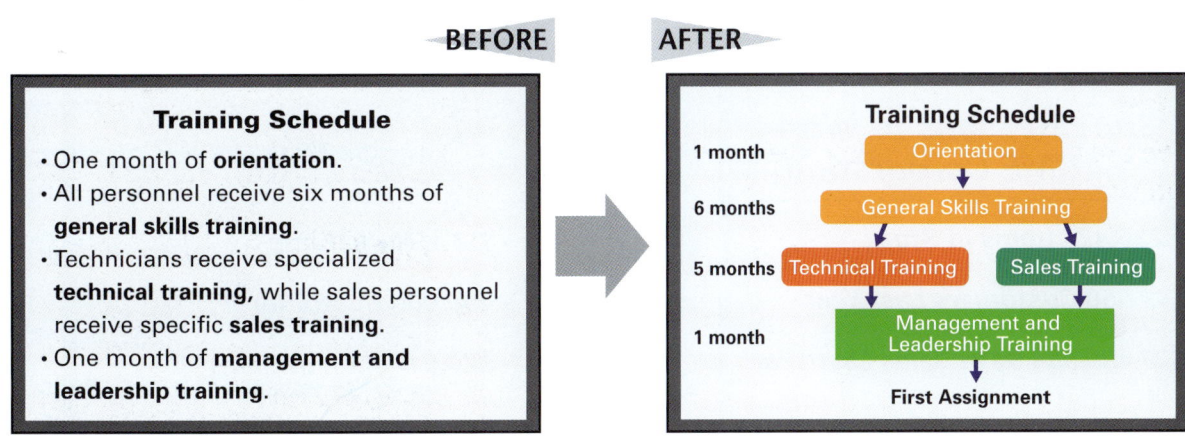

Guideline 2: KISS (Keep your Information Short and Simple)

- *Simplify sentences into easily remembered key words and phrases.*

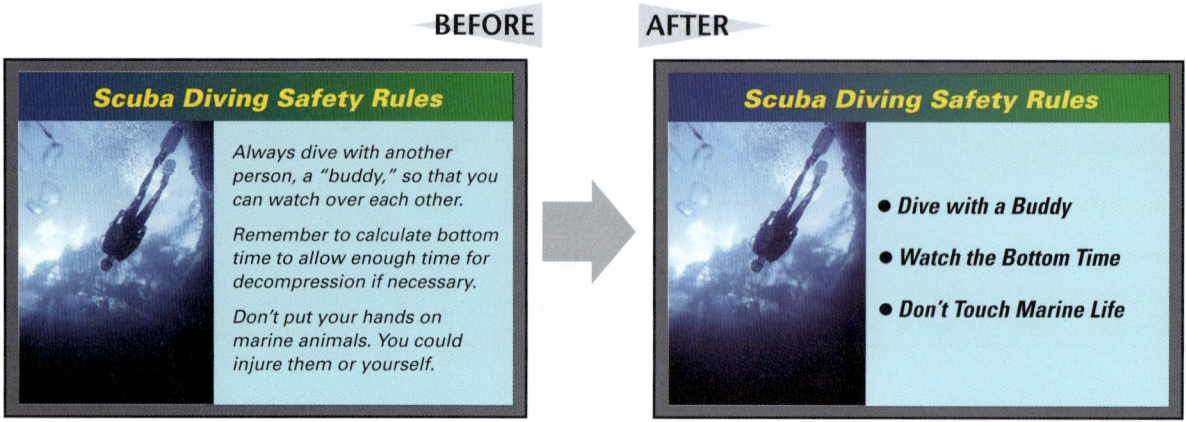

- *Eliminate unnecessary information.*

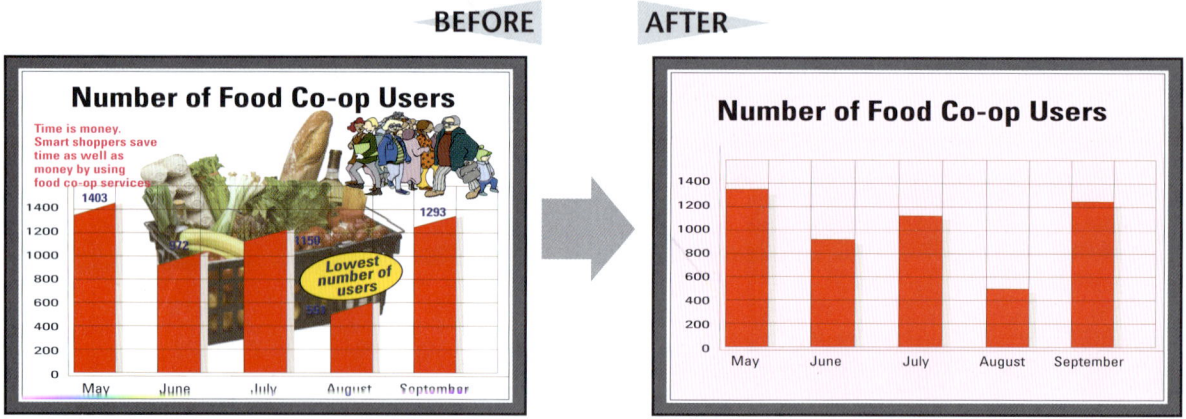

- *Eliminate unnecessary details. Round off numbers and eliminate extra words to make easily remembered key points.*

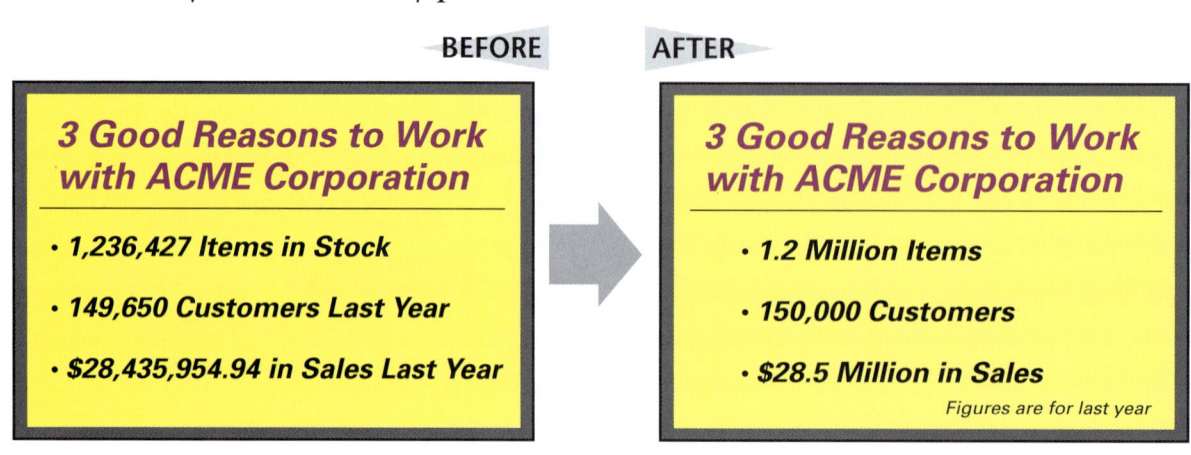

PERFORMANCE

Speech Preparation

Assignment: Prepare a presentation comparing two countries. Your presentation should include a title chart, three data charts, and a chart of questions for you to ask your audience at the end of your presentation.

Step 1 PLAN:
Choose two countries to compare. Do some research for your data charts. For example, you could compare population by age groups, or GNP over the last 5 years.

Step 2 PREPARE:
Design your charts. Use some of the types of visuals from the Glossary of Visuals. Choose the media most appropriate to your information: slides, poster, etc. Use the boxes on the next page for brainstorming.

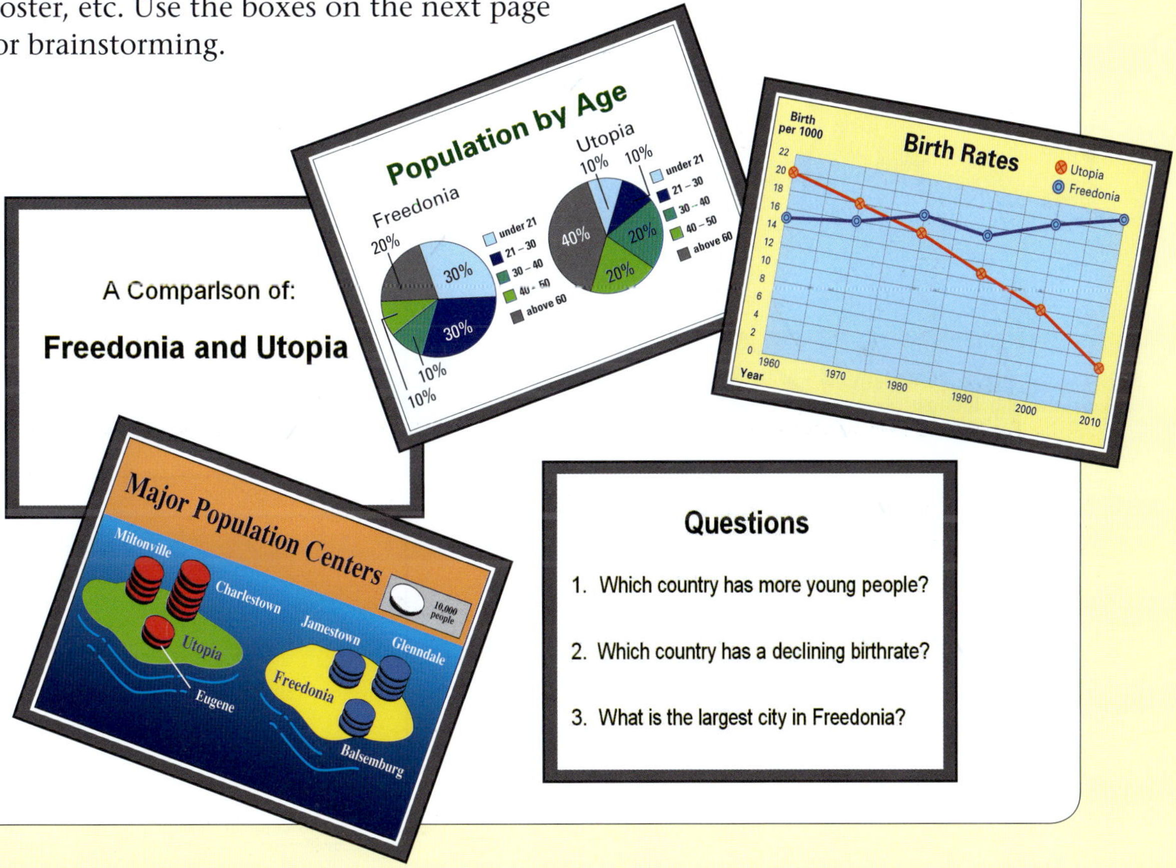

Step 3 PRACTICE:
These visuals will be used in your presentation at the end of the next section, Explaining Visuals.

The Visual Message 49

PERFORMANCE

Brainstorming: It is a good idea to sketch your visuals in pencil before making your final charts. Use the blank charts below to sketch out your visuals.

- **Title chart**
Use the title chart to announce what countries you are comparing.

- **Data charts**
Make three data charts.

- **Question chart**
Make one question about each of your data charts to ask the audience.

Explaining Visuals

FIRST VIEWING:

Watch Presentation 1 of Episode 5 of the DVD. Note how the speaker explains the chart. Close your textbooks and enjoy the speech!

How did she do? Did you notice any problems in her delivery? What problems did you notice in how she explained the visual? Write them below.

_____

_____

_____

SECOND VIEWING:

Watch Presentation 2 of Episode 5. What does the speaker do differently? Close your textbooks and enjoy the speech!

How did she do this time? List the improvements below.

_____

_____

_____

The Visual Message

How to Use Visuals

Look at these common problems of presenting visuals. Have you seen presenters make these mistakes?

Glossary of Presenting Visuals

Problem 1: Standing in front of visual and blocking the audience's view.

Solution: Stand off to the side.

Problem 2: Pointing with the wrong hand.

Solution: Point with the hand closest to the visual.

Problem 3: Not facing the audience.

Solution: Point your toes towards the audience.

Problem 4: Twisting the whole body towards the chart.

Solution: Turn your head, not your body.

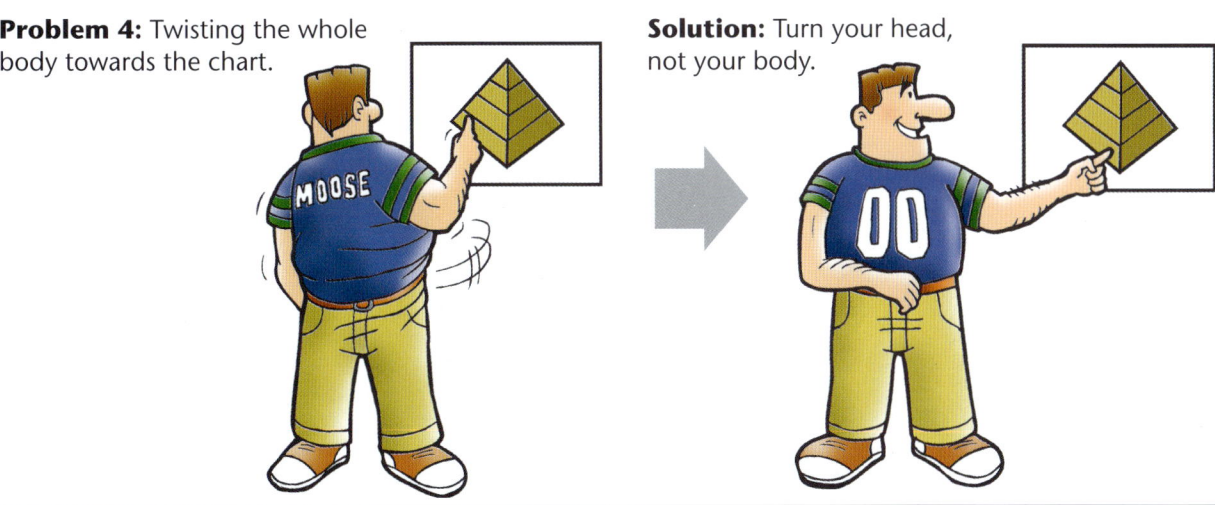

Problem 5: Using the full extent of the pointer.

Solution: Shorten the pointer and stand close to the visual.

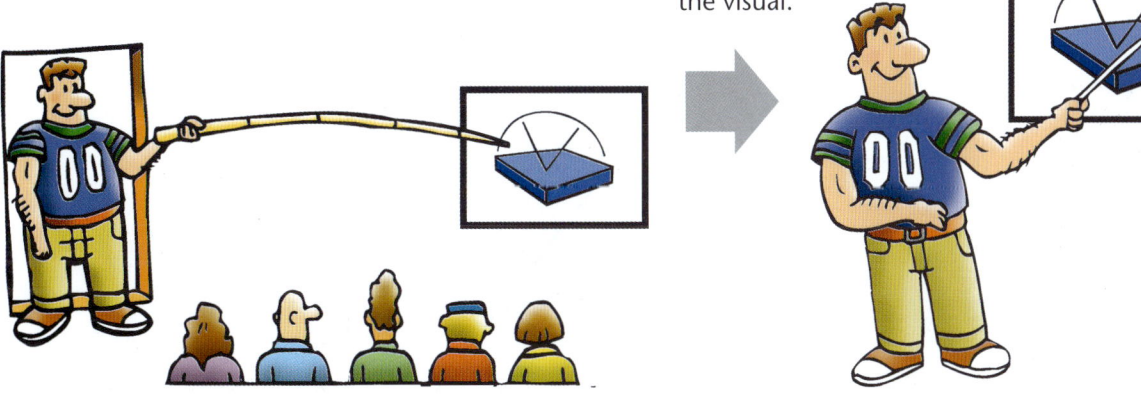

Problem 6: Hitting the screen with the pointer.

Solution: Avoid touching the screen.

How to Explain a Chart

Use I.E.E. (Introduce, Explain and Emphasize) to explain your data charts.

Step 1 INTRODUCE:

First, *introduce* the chart. Tell the audience what kind of chart it is.

"This bar graph shows monthly sales from January to October."

Step 2 EXPLAIN:

Next, *explain* the chart. Tell the audience what is on the chart.

"This axis shows months . . . and this axis shows money in millions."

Step 3 EMPHASIZE:

Finally, *emphasize* what is important on the chart. Tell the audience what to pay attention to.

"The key point on this graph is here, in June, and July, where sales fell."

Glossary of Phrases to Explain a Chart

Step 1 INTRODUCE: Phrases to Introduce the chart

This

Visual	Verb	Indirect Question
pie graph	shows	which automobile is faster.
photograph	describes	where my house is.
flow chart	explains	why product Z is better.
bullet chart		who the managers are.
map		what the functions are.
illustration		what this piece does.
diagram		when production begins.
line graph		how to eat sushi.

Step 2 EXPLAIN: Phrases to Explain the chart

The

Adjective-Noun	Verb	Chart Feature
dotted line	shows	autumn sales.
solid line	describes	population by country.
horizontal axis	represents	printer speed.
vertical axis	stands for	car sales in the U.S.
upper box		numbers of models produced.
lower box		people who traveled abroad.
		speed in miles per hour.

These

Plural Noun	Verb	Chart Feature
dots	show	spring sales.
lines	describe	population by country.
boxes	represent	printer speed.
colors	stand for	sales of products.
figures		different cities.
triangles		new buildings.
		the new features.

Step 3 EMPHASIZE: Phrases to Emphasize key points of the chart

The key point is (that) The point I want you to remember is (that) Please note (that)	• December's sales are the highest, due to Christmas shopping. • all these new features increase the train's speed. • too much salt causes health problems. • air conditioner sales and beer sales increased. • the number of accidents is falling.

The Visual Message

PERFORMANCE

Speech Preparation

Assignment: Now, prepare the explanation for your country comparison speech.

Step 1 — **PREPARE:**
Use I.E.E. (Introduce, Explain and Emphasize) to explain your data charts.

"This chart compares the birthrates of Freedonia and Utopia."

"The right pie graph is Utopia and the left one is Freedonia."

"The key point is . . ."

Step 2 — **PRACTICE:**
Make sure to point at your charts.

Step 3 — **PERFORM:**
Speakers, use your visuals to explain. Listeners, complete the evaluation form on page 103. Fill in the form as in the example below.

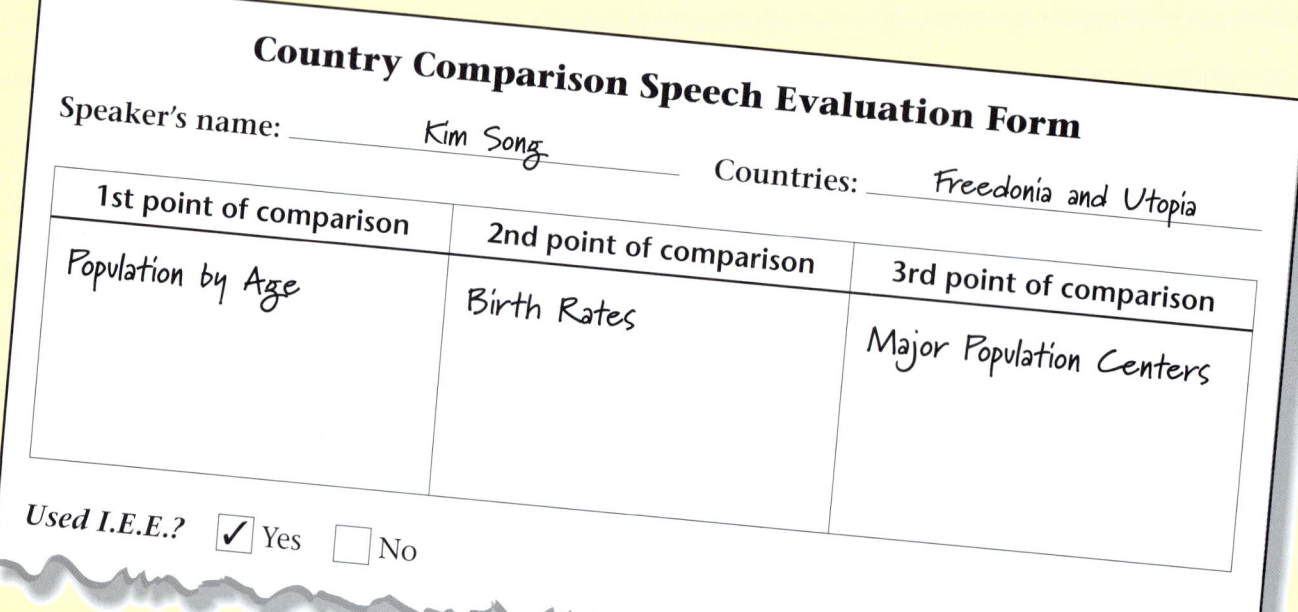

Country Comparison Speech Evaluation Form

Speaker's name: Kim Song
Countries: Freedonia and Utopia

1st point of comparison	2nd point of comparison	3rd point of comparison
Population by Age	Birth Rates	Major Population Centers

Used I.E.E.? ✓ Yes ☐ No

The Story Message

What Is the Story Message?

The Story Message is the way you put your information together into a standard presentation structure.

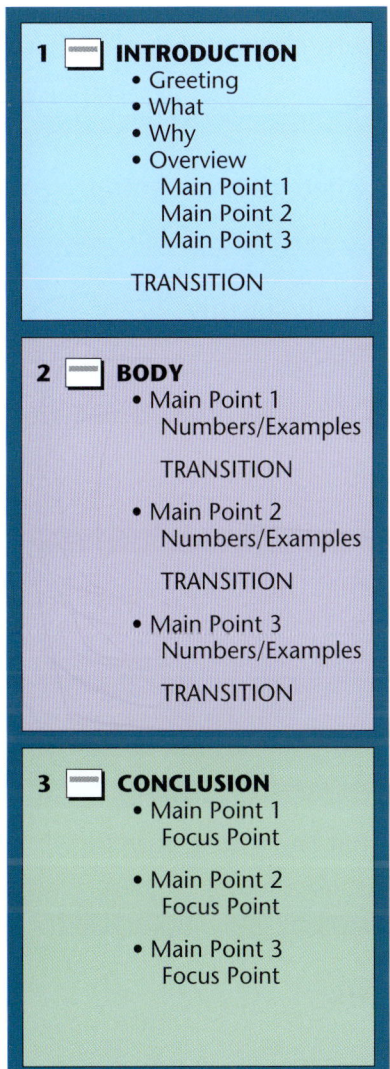

● **The Introduction:**
This is where you get your audience's attention and preview your story.

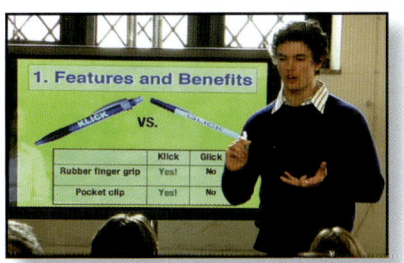

● **The Body:**
This is where transitions connect your visuals into a story.

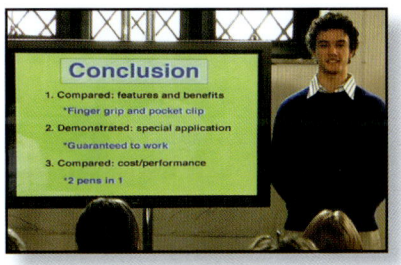

● **The Conclusion:**
This is where you tell your audience what to remember from your story.

Why Is the Story Message Important?

People enjoy stories. People remember stories. A good Story Message makes your presentation interesting, easy to understand, and memorable.

How to Use Presentation Structure

Giving a speech is like giving a tour. Look at the following example of Safari Bob giving a tour of the zoo.

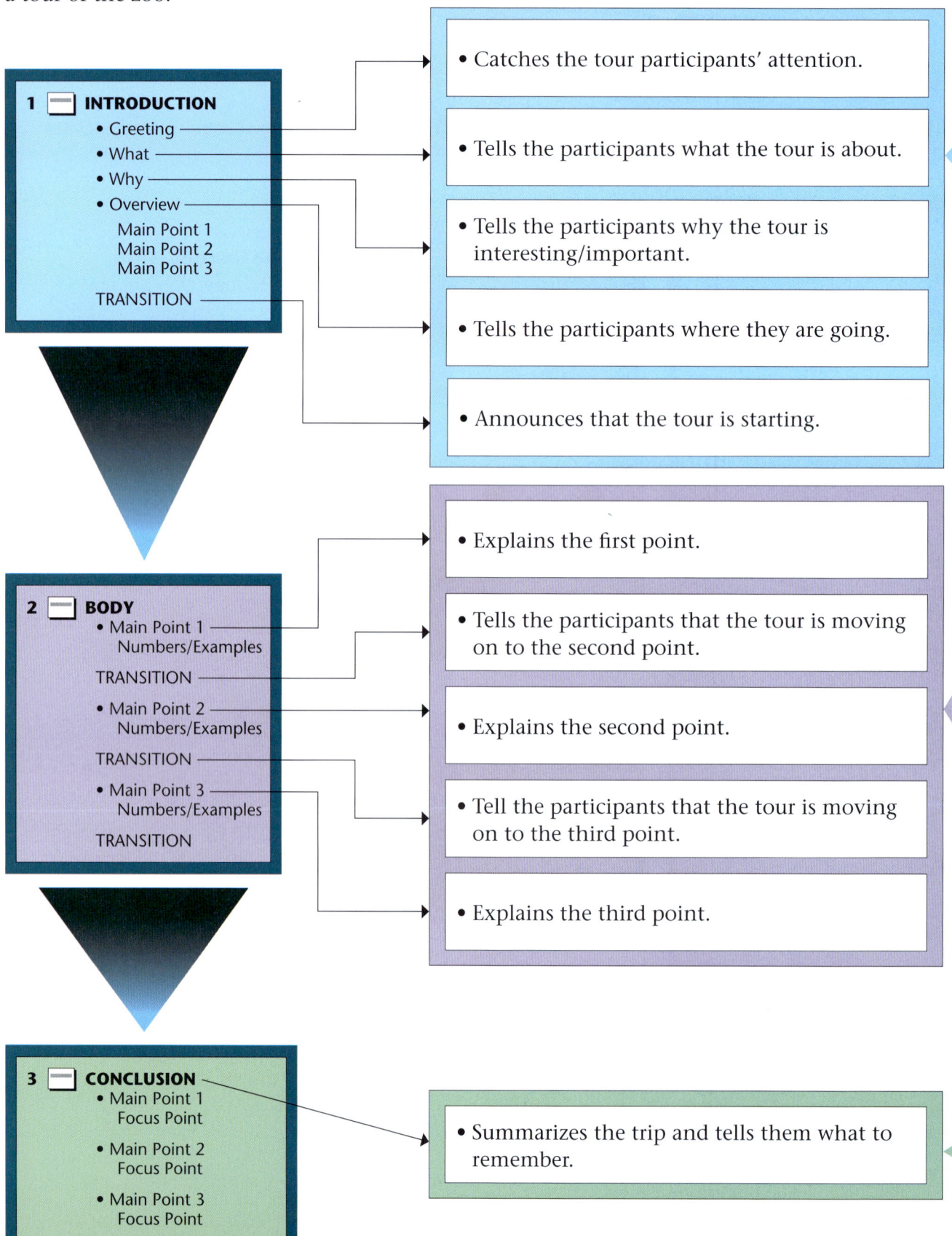

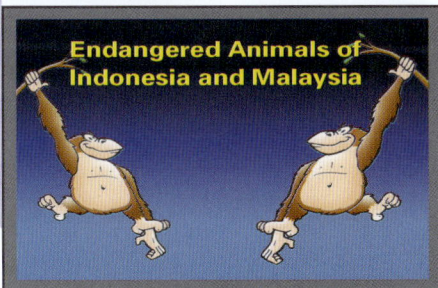
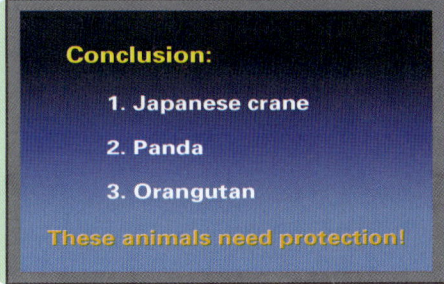

 Good morning! My name is Safari Bob, your tour guide. Today, I have an important message for you. Important because we are going to look at some endangered animals of Asia. These animals may soon disappear without your help.

 Now, as for today's tour. First, we will take a look at the endangered animals of Japan. Second, we will look at the endangered animals of China, and, finally, the endangered animals of Indonesia and Malaysia.

 Here are the endangered animals of Japan. First, the red-crowned crane, sometimes called the Japanese crane . . .

We have seen the endangered animals of Japan. Next, please follow me to the endangered animals of China.

 Here you see the endangered animals of China. Let's begin by taking a look at the Giant Panda . . .

Up to now, we have looked at the endangered animals of both Japan and China. Now, let's move on to the endangered animals of Indonesia and Malaysia.

 Here are the endangered animals of Indonesia and Malaysia. Let's begin by looking at the largest and most famous, the orangutan . . .

 In conclusion, today we saw three groups of animals. First, endangered animals of Japan. Second, endangered animals of China, and third, endangered animals of Indonesia and Malaysia. Thank you for your attention. Do you have any questions?

Practice: Using Presentation Structure

Step 1 So far, we have learned that the structure of a speech is similar to the structure of a tour. We have also seen that the job of a speaker is to guide the audience through the speech. We have learned that a speech has an introduction, a body, and a conclusion.

Now, we will apply all this to making a speech about our favorite restaurant. But, first, let's organize a speech given by the famous pop star, Jennifer Spears, about her favorite restaurant, The Hardly Rock Café. Read and organize the strips in the correct order. The first one is done for you.

	In conclusion, today, I told you two points about the Hardly Rock Café. First, I told you how to get there. Remember to take the "A" train. Second, I told you about the dining experience. Remember to look for my picture, Jennifer Spears, on the wall. Thank you for your attention!
	The Hardly Rock Café is easy to get to. Take the "A" train and get off at Penny Lane. Go straight down Highway Star. The Hardly Rock Café is located next to The House of The Rising Sun.
	First, I'll tell you how to get there, and second I'll tell you about the dining experience.
	Now you know where the Hardly Rock Café is. Next, I'll tell you about the dining experience.
1	Good afternoon! My name is Jennifer Spears. For your next date you should visit the Hardly Rock Café! It is a marvelous place to have a meal with a special friend.
	The food is delicious. I recommend Way Low-Calorie Fruit Salad followed by the Spice Boys Spicy Barbecue Chicken. For dessert, try the Blueberry Hill Cheesecake. While you eat, you can check out all the autographed pictures on the wall. And don't forget to buy one of the unique Hardly Rock Café T-shirts!

Step 2 Listen to the CD and check your answers.

AUDIO 8

Build Your Own Favorite Restaurant Speech

Step 1 How many people can you convince to visit your favorite restaurant? Use the format below to prepare a speech about your favorite restaurant.

Restaurant Recommendation

Introduction

Hello! My name is _____ and you should visit my favorite restaurant, _____.
It is a great place for a meal. ← Why it's important
First, I'm going to tell you about where it is, and second, I'm going to tell you about the menu. ← Overview

Body

My favorite restaurant, _____, is located ← First Point
in _____.
It is near _____.
You can get there by _____
_____.

Now you know where _____ is. Next, I'll tell you what the menu is like. ← Transition

On the drinks menu there is _____, _____, ← Second Point
_____, and _____.
I recommend _____. For your main dish you can order
_____, _____, or _____.
My favorite is _____.
For dessert, you should try _____.

Conclusion

Today, I told you two points about my favorite restaurant _____. ← Summary
First, where it is. Remember _____. ← Reminder
Second, _____. Remember _____.
I hope you will visit the _____ soon!

Step 2 Present your speech in small groups or to the class.

Step 3 After hearing all the speeches, choose the restaurant you would most like to visit.

I would like to visit the restaurant _____, recommended
  _{restaurant name}
by _____.
  _{presenter's name}

The Introduction

What Is the Introduction?

The introduction prepares the audience for your presentation. It tells them what your presentation is about, why it is important, and finally, what to listen for in your speech.

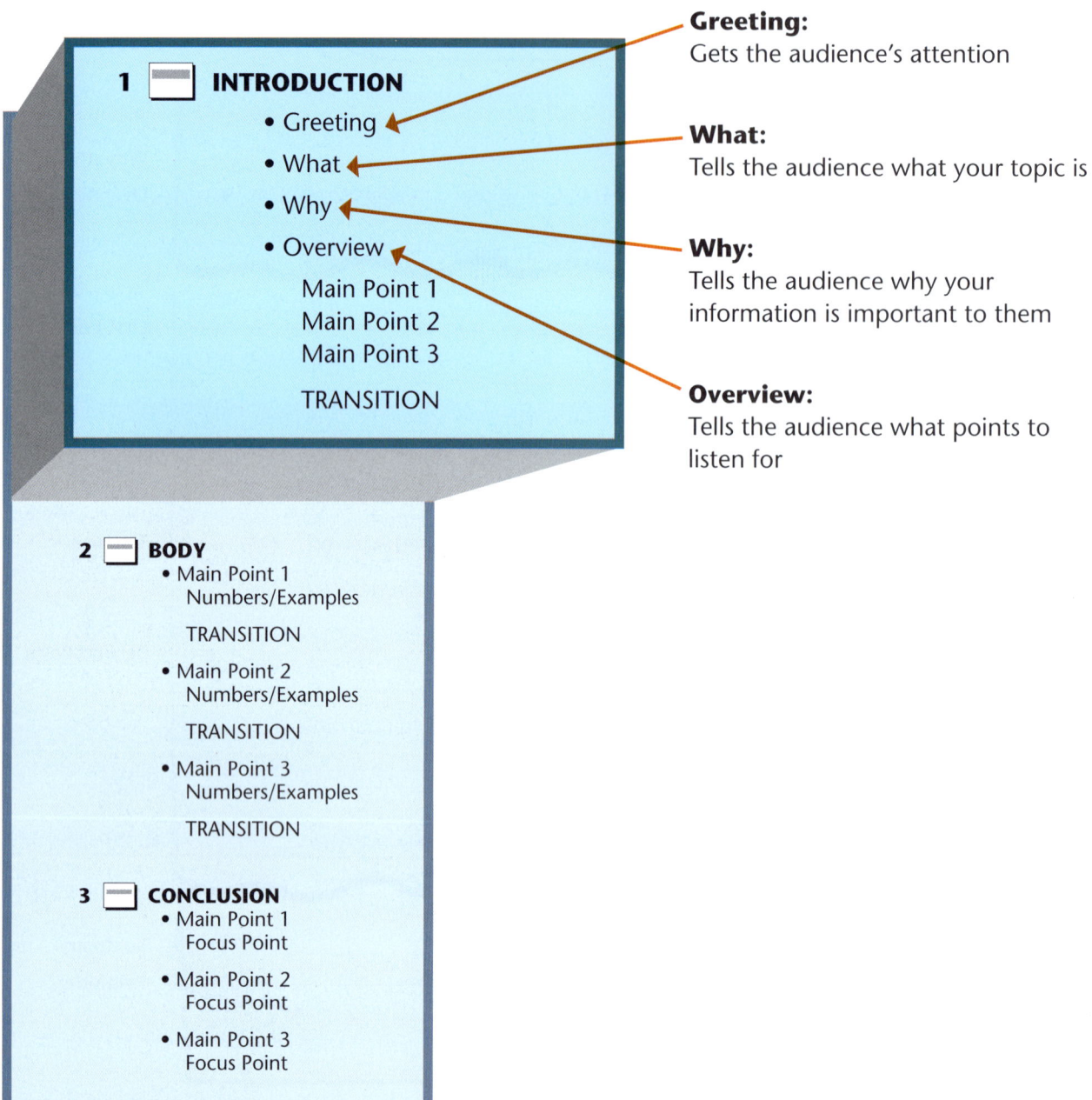

Why Is the Introduction Important?

The introduction is perhaps the most important moment in your presentation. If you get the audience's interest, you have a good chance for success. If you fail to get their interest, they might not listen closely enough to catch your message.

How to Make Introductory Phrases

Glossary of Introductory Phrases

The introduction tells the audience what they are about to hear. Because the actual information comes later, in the body of the speech, you usually use the future tense (will, be going to). You tell the audience the topic you *will* talk about, the reason they *will* want to listen, and the order of the information you *will* present. Look at these four introductions.

THE INTRODUCTION

	1	2	3	4
What	I'm going to talk about... 	I'd like to tell you about... 	I want to describe... 	I will explain to you... 
Why	This information will help you... **FIX YOUR CAR**	After this speech you will be able to... **CARE FOR YOUR DOG**	This (topic) will be important to you because... **THE 2024 OLYMPICS MIGHT BE HELD HERE**	You will need to know this if/because... **YOU HAVE TO COOK DINNER TONIGHT** 
Overview	I'm going to talk about three points. First, I'll tell you about...  Second, I'll tell you about...  Third, I'll tell you about... 	I'll cover three things. To begin with, I'll talk about... **LITTLE DOGS** Next... **MEDIUM SIZED DOGS** Finally... **BIG DOGS**	I'll tell you about three main areas. First of all, I'll tell you...  Then...  Lastly, I'll tell you... 	I have three points that I will describe... To start with, I'll...  After that...  At the end, I'll tell you how to... 

The Story Message 63

How to Recognize Introductory Phrases

 Step 1 Listen to the CD and fill in the blanks.

Good afternoon, I'm Dr. Gourd. Ladies and gentlemen, our planet is in trouble. Today, 1)_____ 2)_____ 3)_____ talk about global warming. 4)_____ is this important for you to know about today? 5)_____ knowing about global warming will help you save the planet. I'm going to cover 6)_____ 7)_____. First, I'm going to talk about the causes of global warming. 8)_____, I'll look at the impact of climate change. Finally, I'll outline what we can do to stop 9)_____ 10)_____.

 Step 2 Listen again, and this time circle the (GREETING), double-underline the WHAT, put the [WHY] in brackets, and underline the whole OVERVIEW.

Practice: Introduction

Step 1 Put the sentences in the correct order. Write the numbers (1–7) on the left. Then circle the (GREETING), double-underline the WHAT, put the [WHY] in brackets, and underline the whole OVERVIEW. The first one is done for you.

	Then, I'm going to tell you about the wet and wild water sports we have planned for you.
1	Welcome aboard!
	To begin with, I'll tell you about the wonderful duty-free shopping available.
	This will help you plan how to spend your five days aboard the Caribbean Queen.
	It's nice to meet all of you. I'm so glad you have chosen Caribbean Adventure Cruises for your summer vacation.
	Lastly, I'll tell you about the treatments available in our beautiful new spa.
	I would like to tell you about all the exciting activities for you to do on board.

 Step 2 Listen to the CD and check your answers.

AUDIO 10

PERFORMANCE

Introduction

SPEECH TYPE:

In Episode 6 of the *Speaking of Speech* DVD, three speakers present the introductions to their persuasive presentations. A persuasive speech presents information to help the audience make a decision. If, at the end of your persuasive speech, the audience agrees with you and is ready and willing to take action, your speech has been a success.

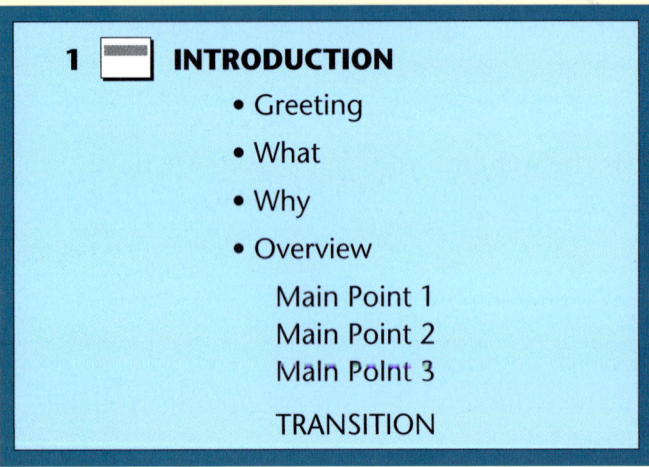

SPEECH SKILL:

In the introduction of your persuasive presentation, you will present the Greeting, the What, the Why, and the Overview.

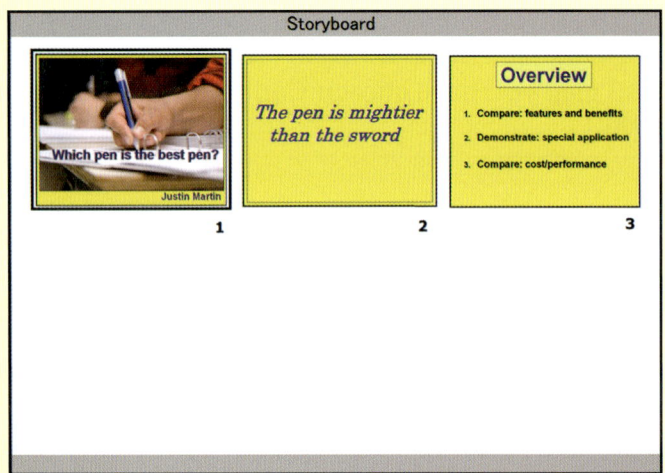

SPEECH PREPARATION:

For this presentation, you will prepare three visuals: a title chart to show the "What," a background chart to explain the "Why," and an overview chart to preview your main points.

Model: Introduction

FIRST VIEWING:

Watch all three introductions in Episode 6 of the DVD. Close your textbook and enjoy the speeches. After viewing, answer these questions.

1. What was the topic of the first speech?
2. What was the topic of the second speech?
3. What was the topic of the third speech?

SECOND VIEWING:

Watch again and fill in the "What," "Why," and "Overview" of each introduction in the table below.

Performance Evaluation Form—Introduction

Speaker's name:	What	Why	Overview
Justin			
Lisa			
Dr. Roberts			

The Story Message

PERFORMANCE

Speech Preparation

Assignment: Choose a product to compare to one or two competing products and show why your choice is better. For example, you could compare two different brands of cameras, or three similar cars made by different companies, or perhaps two electric guitars from different manufacturers. Prepare only the introduction of your product presentation. (In later units you will prepare the body and the conclusion.)

Step 1 PLAN:
Use a storyboard like this to plan the "What," "Why," and "Overview" of your introduction.

Step 2 PREPARE:
Make your charts. You can prepare a computer presentation, make charts on a computer and print them out, or make a poster.

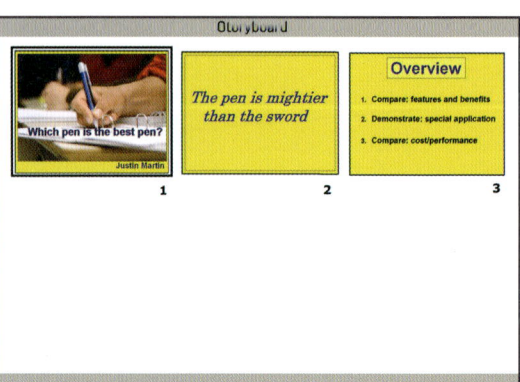

Step 3 PRACTICE:
Practice your introduction. Remember to practice posture, eye contact, gestures, and voice inflection!

Step 4 PERFORM:
Speakers, use your visuals to explain. Listeners, fill in the evaluation form on page 104.

The Body

What Is the Body?

In the introduction, you gave the audience your main points from the overview. In the body, you take each main point and explain it in detail, using evidence. What is evidence? Evidence can be numbers or examples that prove or support your main points.

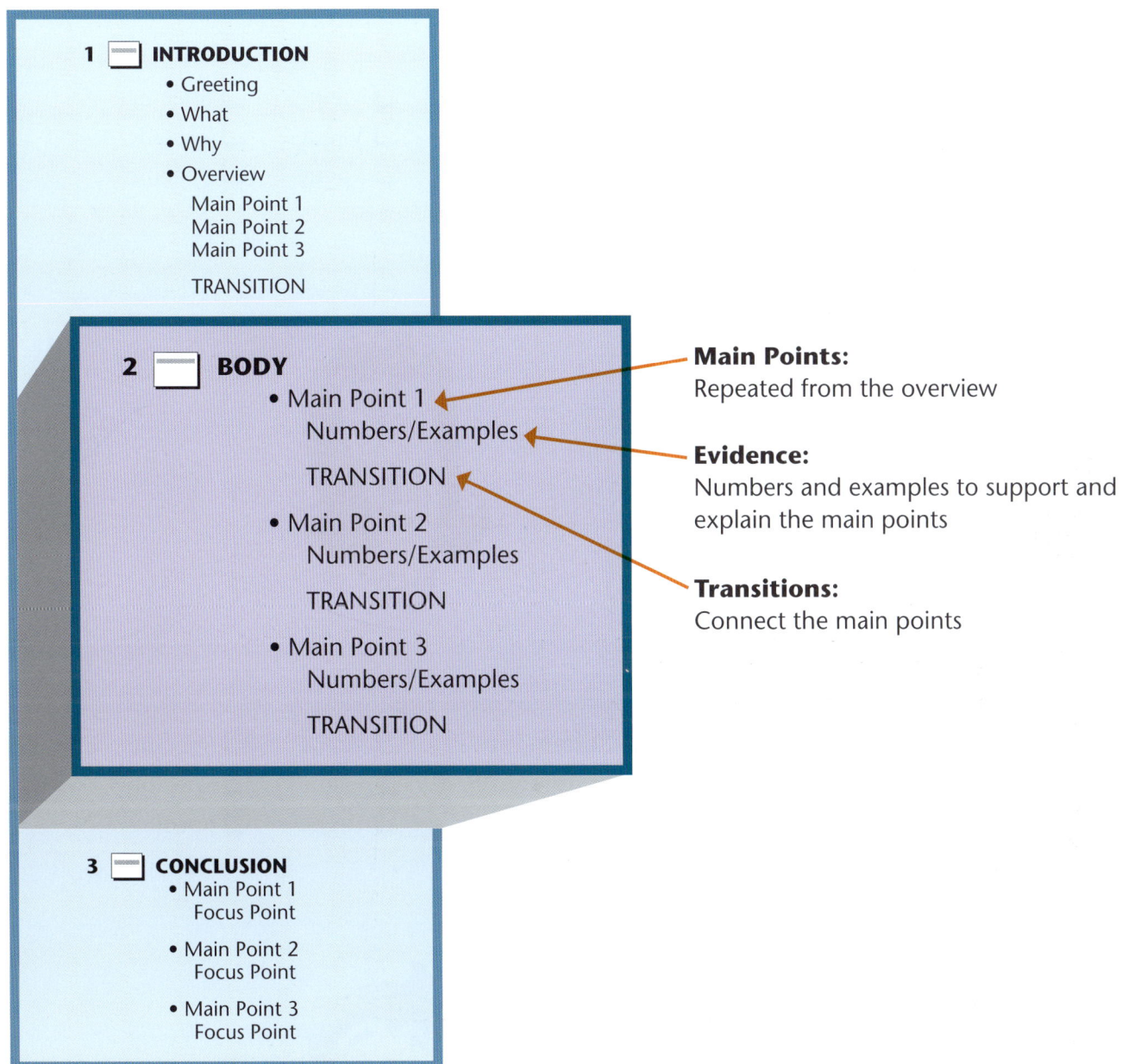

Why Is the Body Important?

The body is the main course of your presentation. Even if you have an interesting appetizer, the introduction, and a tasty dessert, the conclusion, your presentation will fail unless the body is carefully prepared. Prepare the right evidence for the right audience, and prepare clear transitions between your points.

Why Is Evidence in the Body Important?

We use numbers and examples to make our evidence *specific*. When we don't use numbers or examples, our evidence is unclear or *vague*. To be specific, we use either numbers or examples to tell the audience how much, how many, how valuable, how good, how bad, how much better than, how much worse than, etc.

 Listen to the CD and check (✓) whether the evidence is vague or specific.

Statement 1. ❏ Vague ❏ Specific
Statement 2. ❏ Vague ❏ Specific
Statement 3. ❏ Vague ❏ Specific

Statement 4. ❏ Vague ❏ Specific
Statement 5. ❏ Vague ❏ Specific
Statement 6. ❏ Vague ❏ Specific

Statement 7. ❏ Vague ❏ Specific
Statement 8. ❏ Vague ❏ Specific
Statement 9. ❏ Vague ❏ Specific

Statement 10. ❏ Vague ❏ Specific
Statement 11. ❏ Vague ❏ Specific
Statement 12. ❏ Vague ❏ Specific

How to Use Evidence in the Body

Numbers are usually used as evidence when we are talking about prices, percentages, statistics, sizes, distances, lengths of time, or other things that are easily measured. Examples are usually used as evidence when we are talking about quality, comfort, beauty or other things that are difficult to measure.

AUDIO 12 Listen to the CD and check whether the speaker uses a number or an example as evidence.

1. Number ☐ Example ☐ — "The price of this sewing machine is . . ."

2. "You can believe our quality is high because . . ." — Number ☐ Example ☐

3. Number ☐ Example ☐ — "Prices are high in the city . . ."

4. "It is easy to get lost in my neighborhood . . ." — Number ☐ Example ☐

5. Number ☐ Example ☐ — "That rookie has had a great year . . ."

6. "Research shows that cigarette smokers are . . ." — Number ☐ Example ☐

The Story Message

Practice: Using Evidence in the Body

Now try giving numbers and examples as evidence yourself. Write three pieces of evidence for the following statements. Use either numbers or examples. (If you don't know real numbers or examples, it is OK to guess.)

My hometown is beautiful.

1. _____
2. _____
3. _____

My university is a great school.

1. _____
2. _____
3. _____

Practice: Using Evidence in the Body—Pairwork

Student A (Student B: Please turn to the next page.)

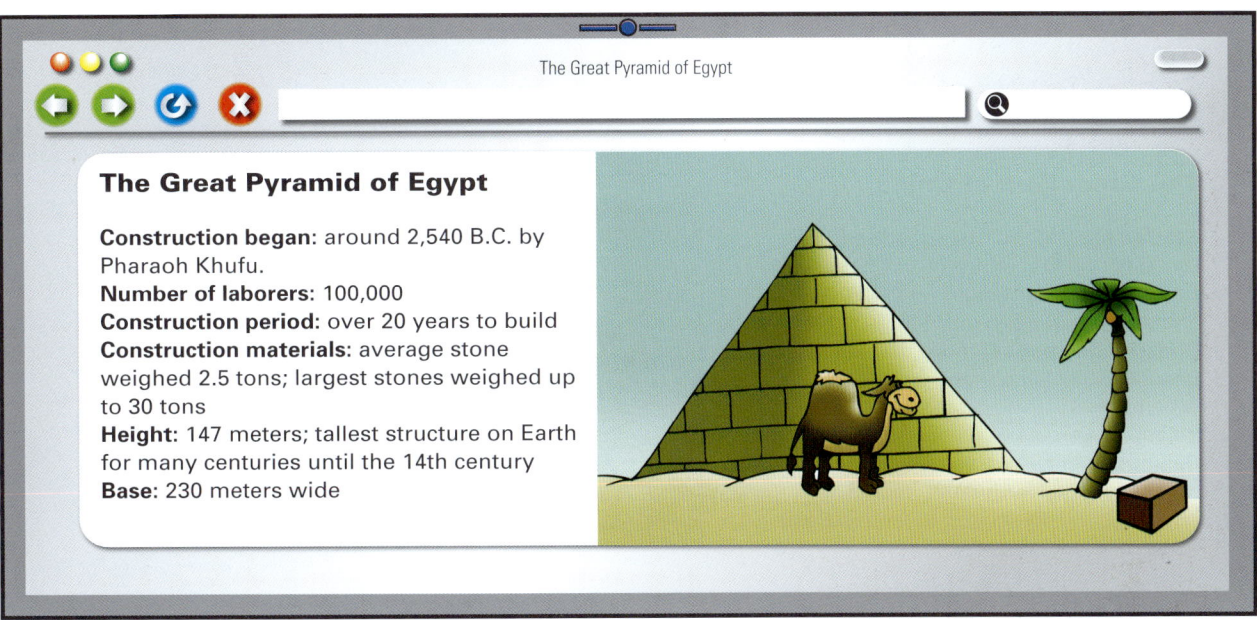

The Great Pyramid of Egypt

Construction began: around 2,540 B.C. by Pharaoh Khufu.
Number of laborers: 100,000
Construction period: over 20 years to build
Construction materials: average stone weighed 2.5 tons; largest stones weighed up to 30 tons
Height: 147 meters; tallest structure on Earth for many centuries until the 14th century
Base: 230 meters wide

Step 1 **Prepare:** Look at the web page above. Write two pieces of evidence to support each statement about the Great Pyramid of Egypt.

    Statement: The Great Pyramid of Egypt is very large.
        Evidence: _____
        Evidence: _____

    Statement: The Great Pyramid of Egypt is very old.
        Evidence: _____
        Evidence: _____

    Statement: The Great Pyramid of Egypt was very difficult to construct.
        Evidence: _____
        Evidence: _____

Step 2 **Present:** Give a short speech on the Great Pyramid to your partner. Use the statements and the supporting evidence. When you have finished, ask your partner three questions about your speech.

Step 3 **Listen:** Listen as your partner makes a short speech on the Great Wall of China. Make notes and be ready to answer three questions.

Practice: Using Evidence in the Body—Pairwork

Student B

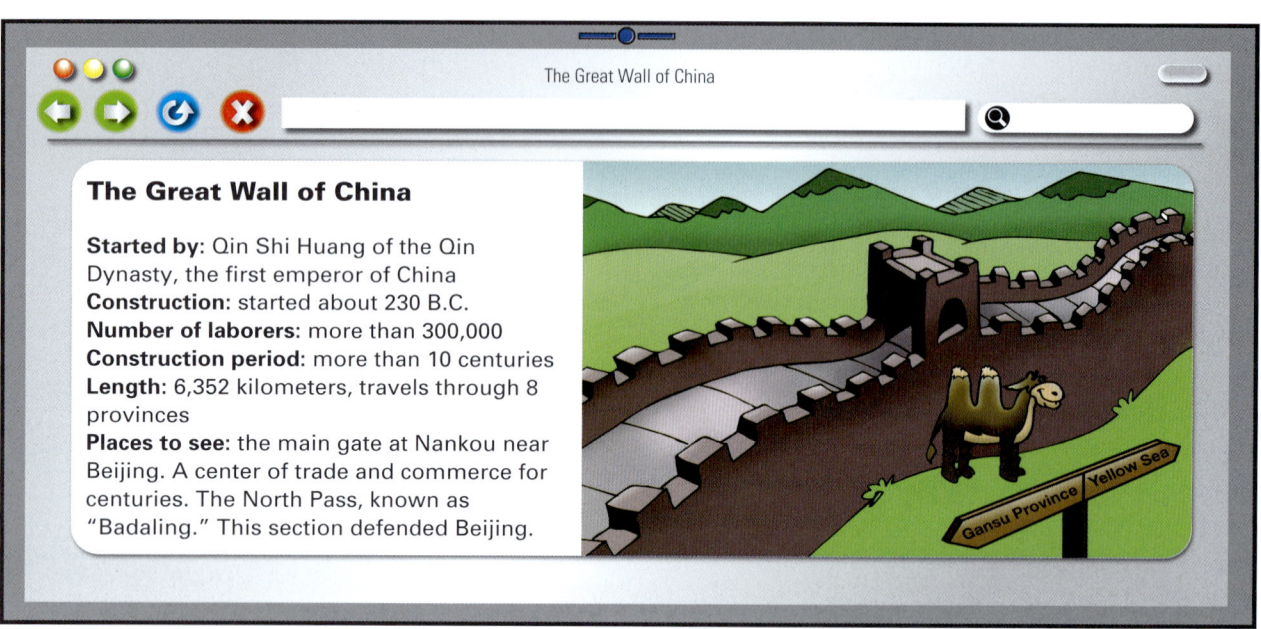

Step 1 **Prepare:** Look at the web page above. Write two pieces of evidence to support each statement about the Great Wall of China.

Statement: The Great Wall of China is very long.
Evidence: _____
Evidence: _____

Statement: The Great Wall of China is very old.
Evidence: _____
Evidence: _____

Statement: There are many interesting places to visit along the Great Wall of China.
Evidence: _____
Evidence: _____

Step 2 **Listen:** Listen as your partner makes a short speech on the Great Pyramid of Egypt. Make notes and be ready to answer three questions.

Step 3 **Present:** Next, give a short speech on the Great Wall of China to your partner. Use the statements and the supporting evidence. When you have finished, ask your partner three questions about your speech.

What Are Transitions and Sequencers?

In this tour around the islands, the tour guide uses word bridges called transitions and sequencers. Transitions are the large bridges, e.g. *After we have talked about . . .* , etc. Sequencers are small bridges, e.g. *first, next, after*. These words connect information within each main point of your speech.

Listen to the CD and trace the route of the tour with your finger. By listening to the transitions and sequencers, you should know exactly where you are at all times.

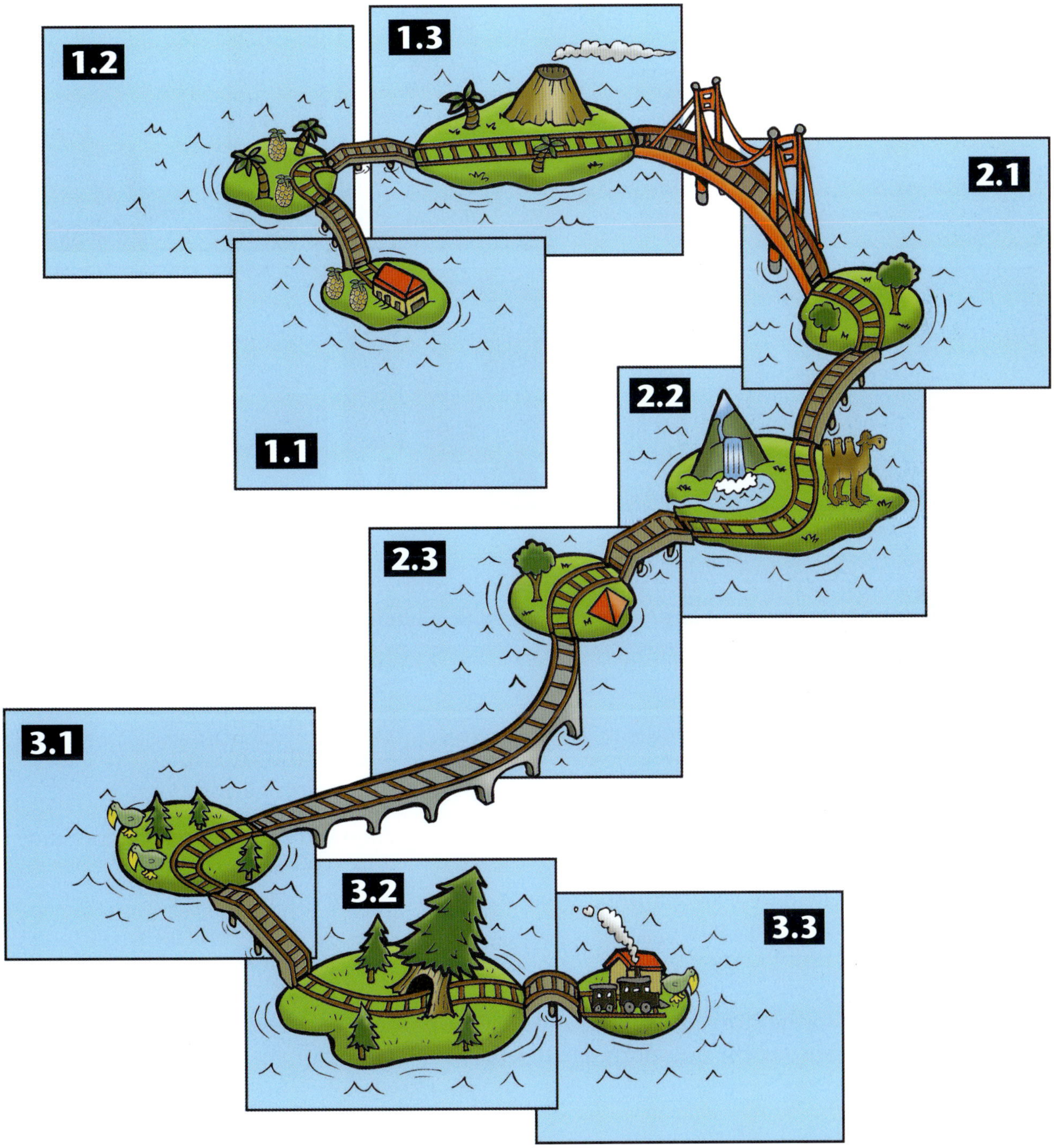

The Story Message

Why Are Transitions and Sequencers Important?

Step 1 Listen to the story told without transitions or sequencers; then try to answer the questions below. Mark your answers with a circle.

AUDIO 14

1. Where is the taxi in picture 2 going?
    a. To the hotel
    b. To the beach
    c. To the airport
    d. I don't know.

2. Where is the restaurant in picture 3?
    a. In the hotel
    b. At the beach
    c. In the airport
    d. I don't know.

3. Who is the girl in picture 5?
    a. The man's daughter
    b. The mayor's daughter
    c. The man's wife
    d. I don't know.

4. When did the man get the present?
    a. The next week
    b. After lunch
    c. The next morning
    d. I don't know.

Step 2 Listen to the story again. This time the story includes transitions and sequencers. Try to answer the questions again. This time mark your answers with a triangle.

AUDIO 15

Speaking of Speech New Edition

How to Use Transitions

Here are two simple patterns for building transitions. The first pattern, numbers 1 through 4, is *Past/Future*. The second pattern, numbers 5 through 8, is *Statement/Rhetorical Question*. Practice these with a partner.

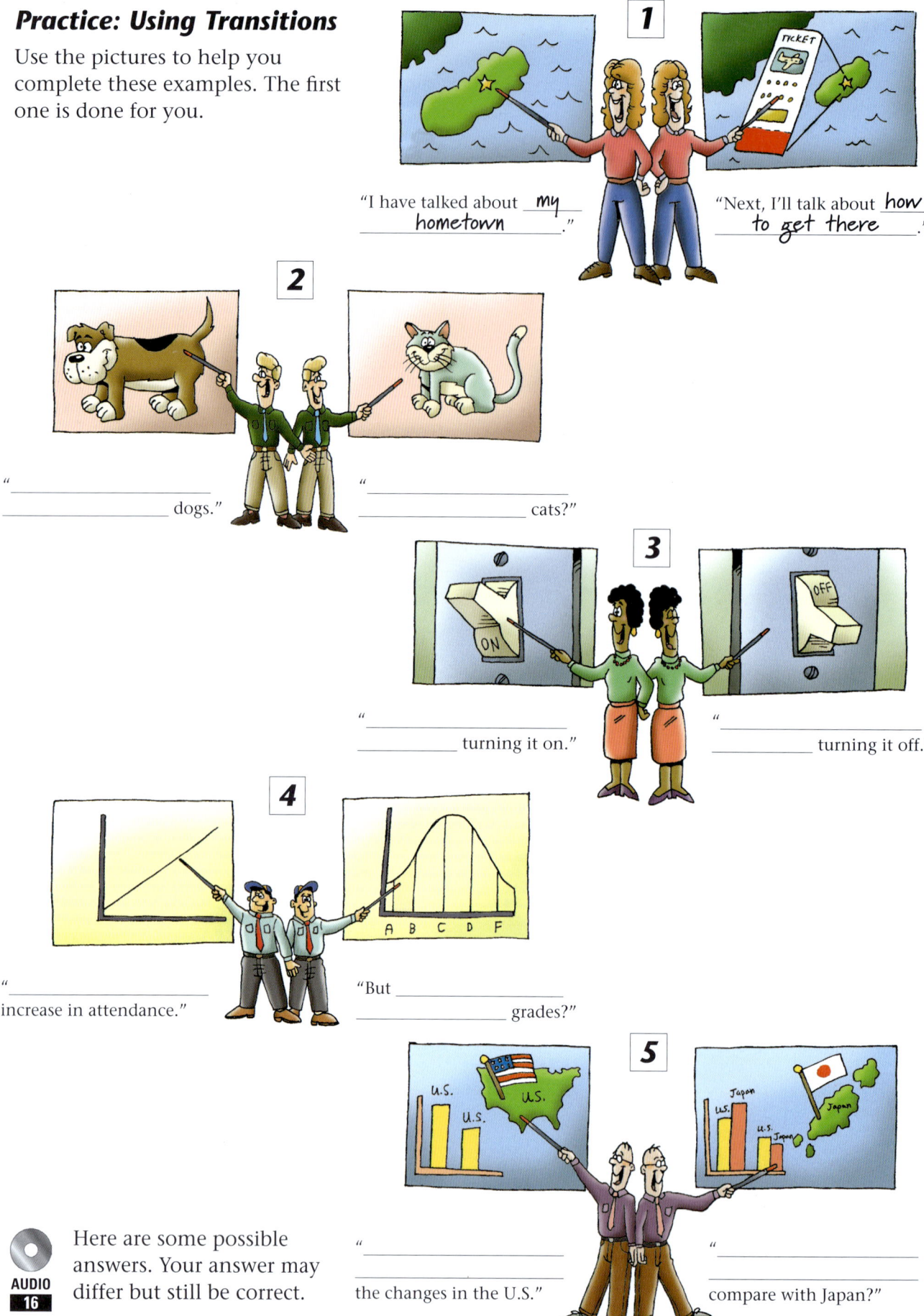

How to Recognize Transitions and Sequencers

 Listen to the demonstration speech about how to make a BLT (bacon, lettuce, and tomato) sandwich. Write sequencers (e.g. first, then, next, after that, now) between the actions in the pictures below. Write transitions in the large boxes.

Today, I'll tell you how to make a BLT sandwich.

1. fry two pieces of bacon at medium heat

First

2. toast two pieces of bread

3. spread butter and mayonnaise on the toast

4. slice a tomato

5. cut the lettuce

6. put the bacon on the toast

7. put on the lettuce and tomato slices

8. cover with the other piece of toast

9. serve with potato chips

Enjoy!

The Story Message

Practice: Using Transitions and Sequencers—Pairwork

 **Student A**   Look at this page and page 81. *(Student B: Please turn to pages 82 and 83.)*

Speaker's Page

Step 1 Write sequencers between the actions in the pictures below.
Step 2 Write transitions in the long boxes. (Use page 77 to help you with the transitions.)
Step 3 Read your recipe to your partner.
Step 4 Listen to your partner and complete page 81.

Listener's Page

Listen to your partner's recipe. Write the transitions that your partner reads in the long boxes and write the sequencers in the boxes between the actions.

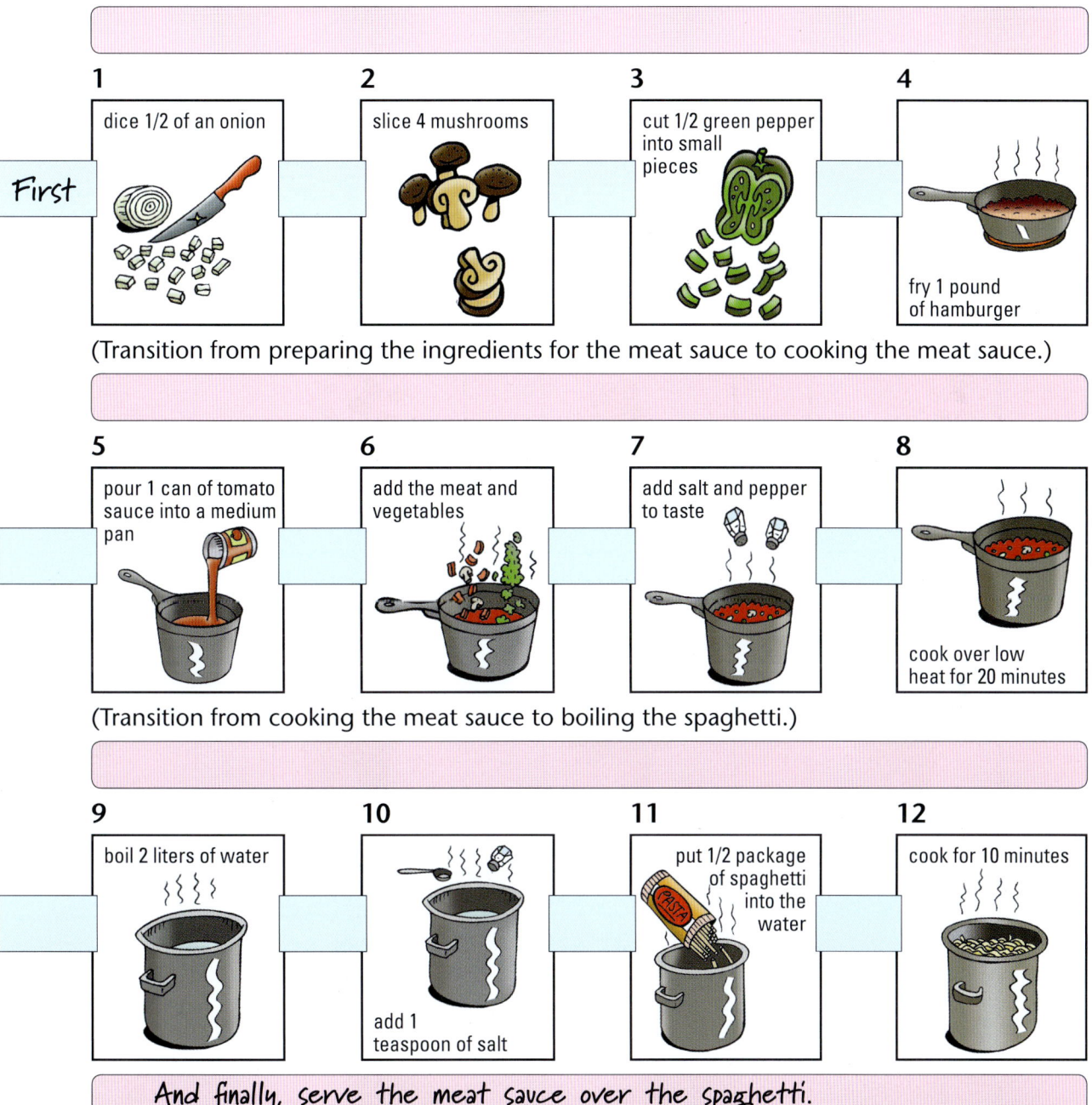

Practice: Using Transitions and Sequencers—Pairwork

 Look at this page and page 83.

Speaker's Page

Step 1 Write sequencers between the actions in the pictures below.

Step 2 Write transitions in the long boxes. (Use page 77 to help you with the transitions.)

Step 3 Listen to your partner and complete page 83.

Step 4 Read your recipe on this page to your partner.

(Transition from preparing the ingredients for the meat sauce to cooking the meat sauce.)

(Transition from cooking the meat sauce to boiling the spaghetti.)

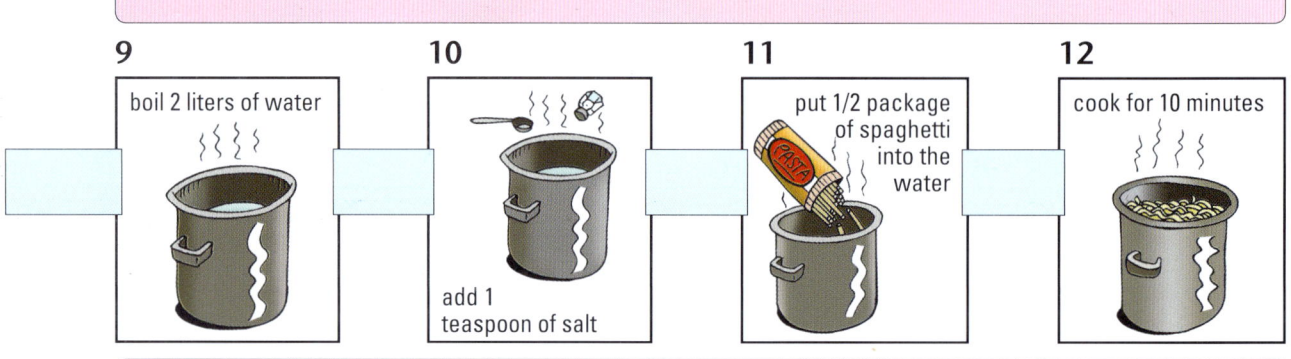

Listener's Page

Listen to your partner's recipe. Write the transitions that your partner reads in the long boxes and write the sequencers in the boxes between the actions.

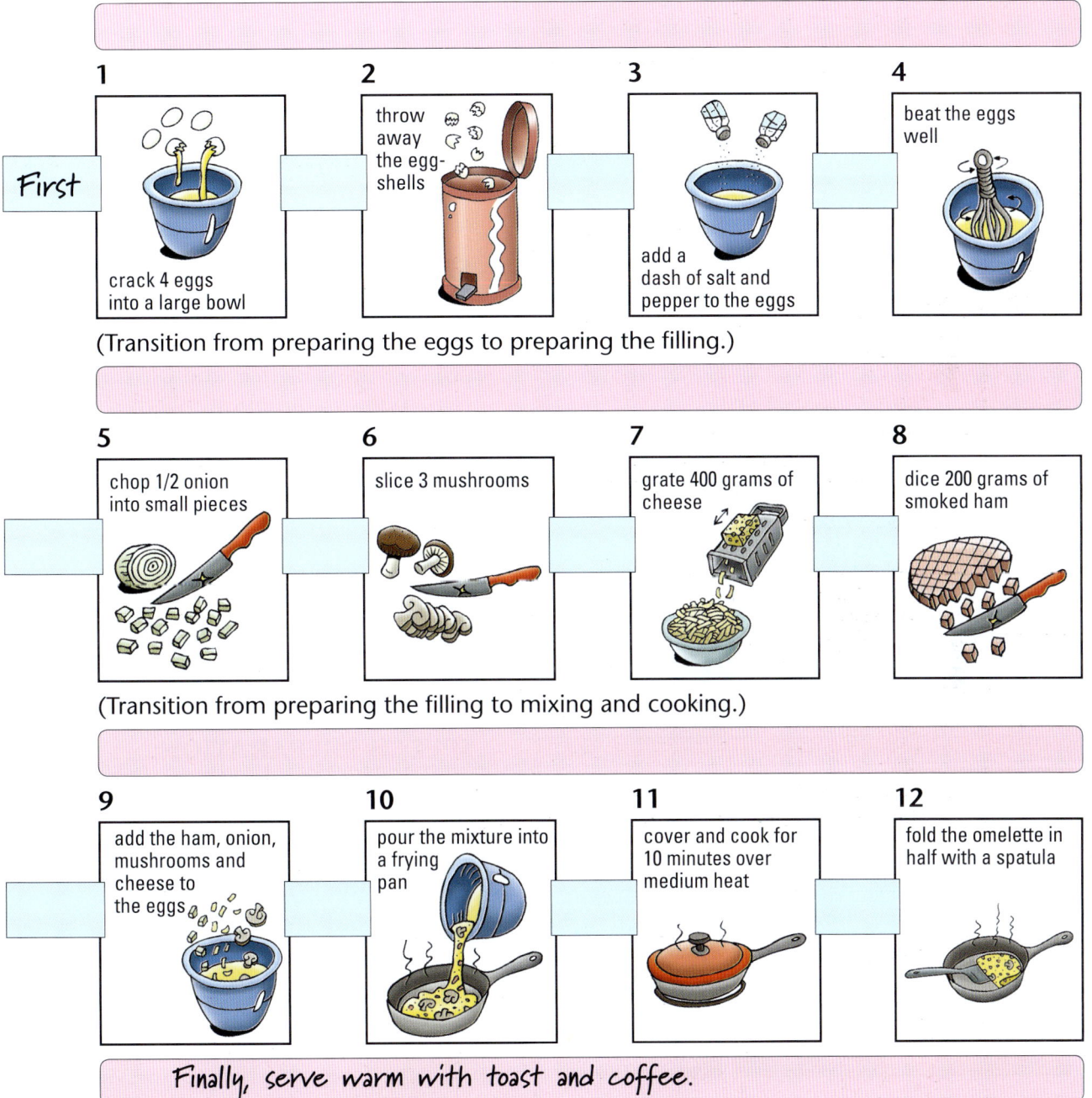

(Transition from preparing the eggs to preparing the filling.)

(Transition from preparing the filling to mixing and cooking.)

Finally, serve warm with toast and coffee.

PERFORMANCE

Body

SPEECH TYPE:

In Episode 7 of the *Speaking of Speech* DVD, Justin presents the body of his persuasive presentation. One of the best ways to win agreement and action from your audience is to make comparisons. For example, Justin compares his two-color pen to a single-color pen to highlight the advantages of his product.

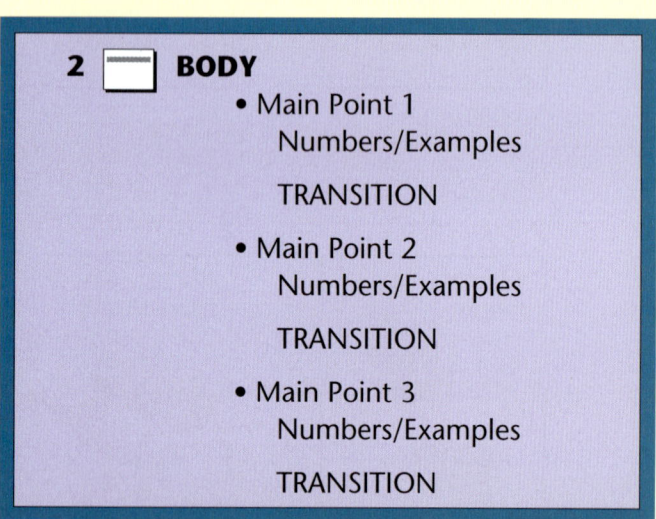

SPEECH SKILL:

In the body of your persuasive presentation, you will present the main points with evidence, and use transitions to tie your presentation together.

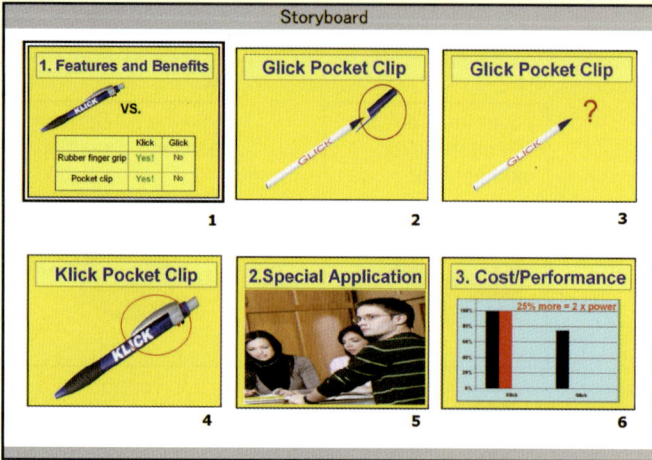

SPEECH PREPARATION:

For this presentation, you will prepare at least one visual to explain each main point in the body of your persuasive presentation.

Model: Body

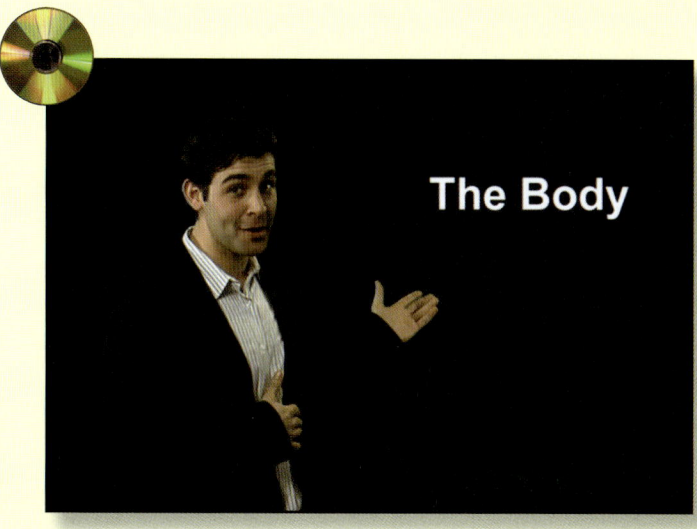

FIRST VIEWING:

Watch Episode 7 of the DVD. Close your textbooks and enjoy the speech! After viewing, answer these questions:

1. What product is he presenting?
2. How many points are in the body of his presentation?

SECOND VIEWING:

Watch again and fill out the evaluation form below. Write the contents of the slides in the boxes, and write the transition under the slide. The first one is done for you.

Performance Evaluation Form—Body

Speaker's name: _____

Product: _____

1. Features and benefits

   Transition: _the second feature is the pocket clip_

2. _____

   Transition: _____

3. _____

   Transition: _____

4. _____

   Transition: _____

5. _____

   Transition: _____

The Story Message 85

PERFORMANCE

Speech Preparation

Assignment: Prepare the body of your product presentation. (In the next unit you will prepare the conclusion.)

Step 1

PLAN:
Use a storyboard like this to plan the charts for the body of your presentation. Write your transition under each chart.

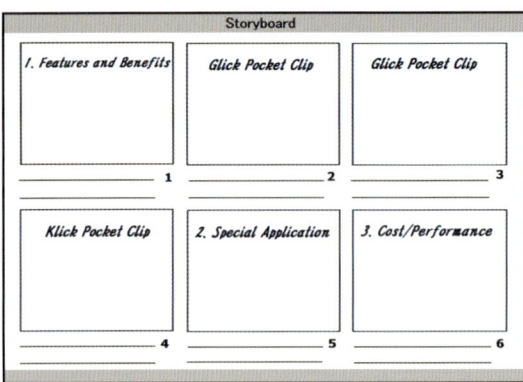

Step 2

PREPARE:
Make your charts. You can prepare a computer presentation, make charts on a computer and print them out, or make a poster.

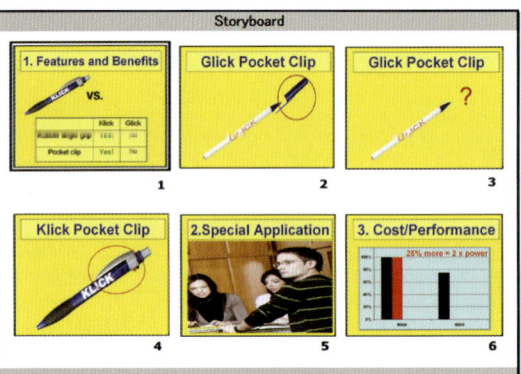

Step 3

PRACTICE:
Practice the body. Think about how to **Introduce**, **Explain**, **Emphasize** each chart, and how to **Transition** from chart to chart.

Step 4

PERFORM:
Speakers, present the body of your product presentation. Listeners, fill in the evaluation form on page 105.

The Conclusion

What Is the Conclusion?

The conclusion is your final message to the audience. It both *summarizes* the presentation and *emphasizes* what you want the audience to remember. The conclusion *summarizes* the presentation by repeating the main points from the overview in the introduction. The conclusion *emphasizes* by repeating some key numbers or examples from each point in the body of your speech.

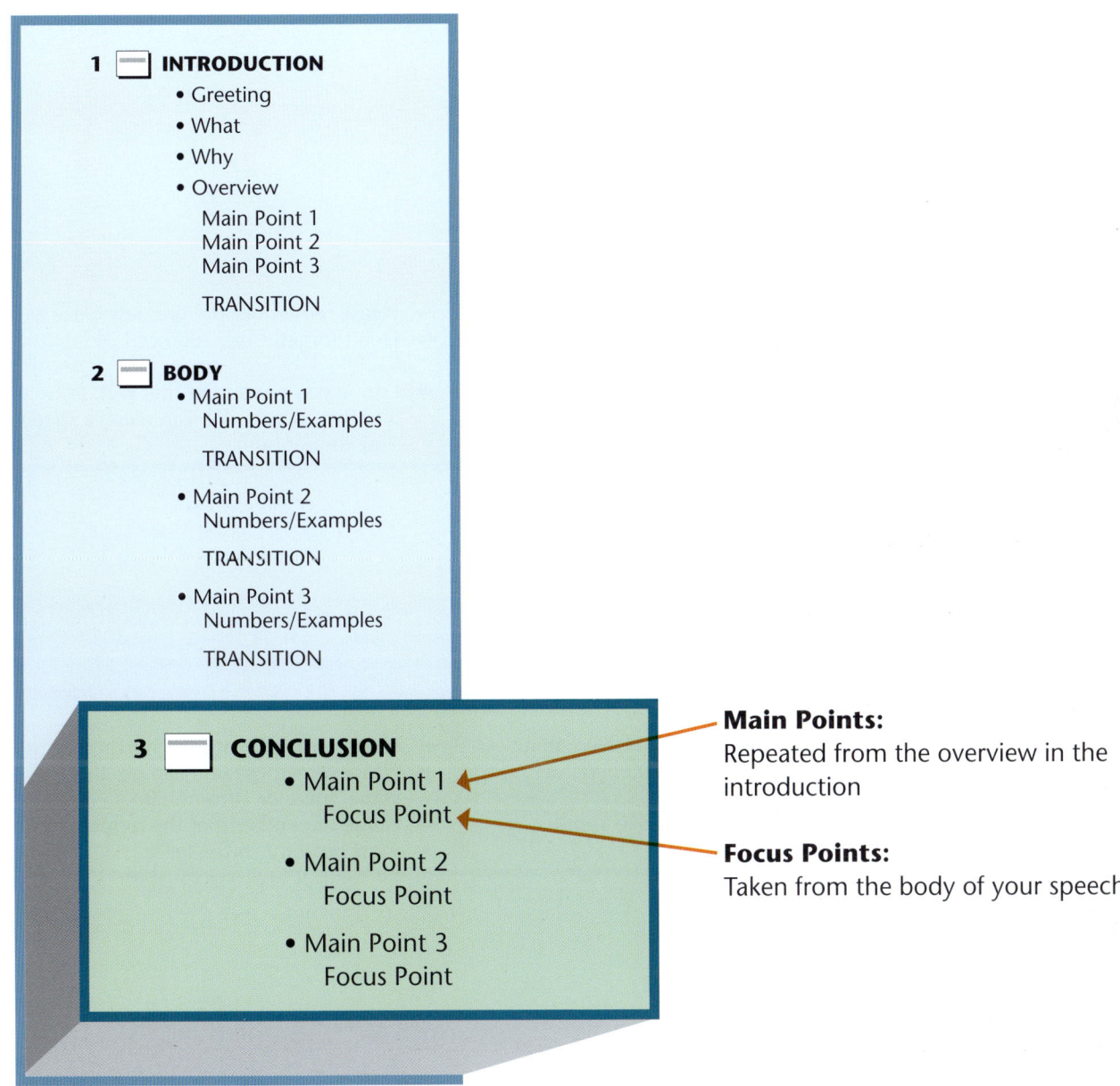

Main Points: Repeated from the overview in the introduction

Focus Points: Taken from the body of your speech

Why Is the Conclusion Important?

The conclusion is your last chance to tell your audience what you want them to remember. It also prepares the audience for the question and answer session.

The Story Message

How to Make a Conclusion

- Remember that in the introduction, verbs are in the *future* tense (will, be going to, etc.) because you are going to speak about the main points to follow in the body.
- Then, in the body, verbs are in the *present* tense (are, is, does, takes, makes, etc.).
- Now, in the conclusion, verbs in the *past* tense are used because you are summarizing what you spoke about in the body.

Glossary of Conclusion Phrases

In the Overview you said:	Body	In the Conclusion, you should say:	Add numbers and examples from the Body
I'm going to talk about three points. First, I'll tell you about the tires. Second, I'll tell you how powerful the engine is. Third, I'll tell you about the speed of this combination.	Numbers and Examples	I talked about three points. First, I told you about the tires. Second, I told you about how powerful the engine is. Third, I told you about the speed of this combination.	→ Please remember the tires last twice as long. → Don't forget it has 2000 cc. → I hope you remember that with these tires and this engine, you can reach a speed of 200 km per hour.
I have three points that I will describe. First of all, I will talk about . . . Then, I'm going to describe . . . Lastly, I'll tell you about . . .	Numbers and Examples	I had three points that I described. First of all, I talked about . . . Then, I described . . . Lastly, I spoke about . . .	→ Please remember it's the northernmost city. → Please remember you can get there by plane, train, or automobile. → Please remember that the mountains are the most beautiful in the fall.
I will cover four points. To begin with . . . Next, I'll tell you about . . . After that, I'll speak about . . . Finally, I will talk about . . .	Numbers and Examples	I covered four points. I began with . . . Next, told you about . . . After that, I spoke about . . . Finally, I talked about . . .	→ Don't forget . . . → Please remember . . . → I hope you'll remember . . . → Remember . . .

Practice: Conclusion Pairwork

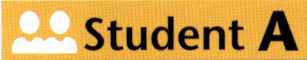 **Student A**   (Student B: Please turn to the next page.)

Step 1 Use the information from the outline to complete the focus points on the e-phone conclusion slide below.

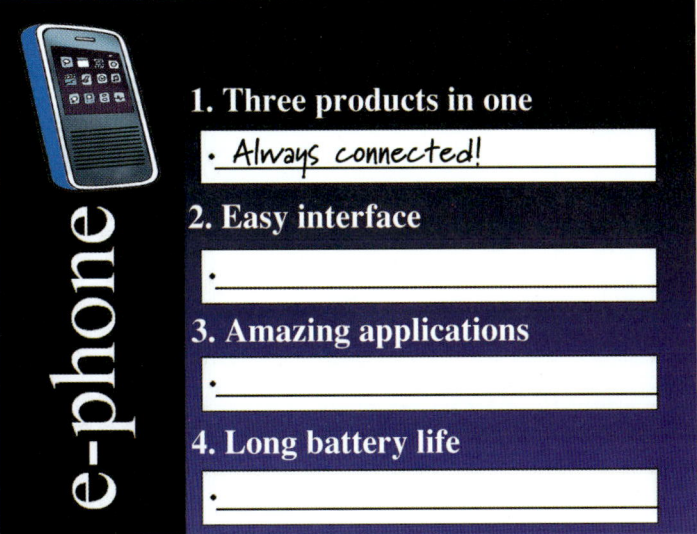

e-phone
1. Three products in one
   • Always connected!
2. Easy interface
   •
3. Amazing applications
   •
4. Long battery life
   •

Step 2 Use your e-phone conclusion slide to present the conclusion to your partner.

Step 3 Listen to your partner and complete the e-guitar conclusion slide.

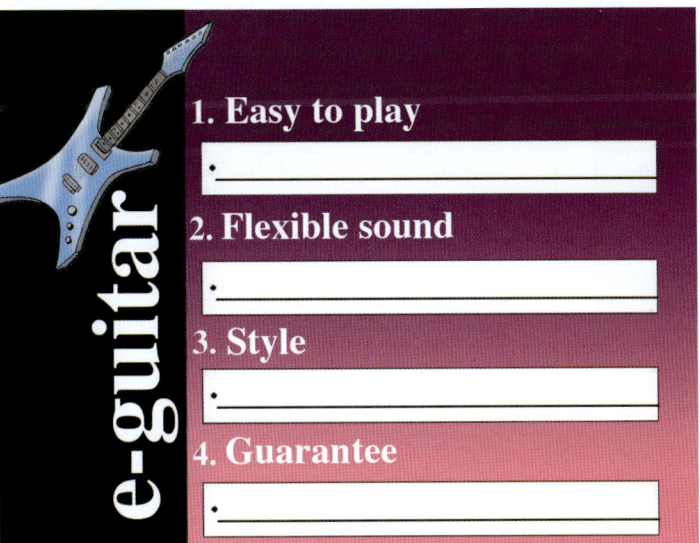

e-guitar
1. Easy to play
   •
2. Flexible sound
   •
3. Style
   •
4. Guarantee
   •

☐ **Overview:**
  1. Three products in one
  2. Easy interface
  3. Amazing applications
  4. Long battery life

☐ **1. Three Products in One**
  • Phone
  • Internet browser
  • e-Pod
  Remember: "Always connected!"

☐ **2. Easy Interface**
  • Touchscreen typing
  • Large, 4-inch screen
  • Rightway Technology automatically adjusts view of screen
  Remember: Touchscreen typing

☐ **3. Amazing Applications**
  • Has 30 applications including weather and maps
  • Over 2,000 free downloadable games
  Remember: 2,000 free games

☐ **4. Long Battery Life**
  • 100 hours between charges
  • 3-year guarantee
  Remember: 100 hours per charge

The Story Message

Practice: Conclusion Pairwork

 **Student B**

Step 1 Use the information from the outline to complete the focus points on the e-guitar conclusion slide below.

e-guitar
1. Easy to play
2. Flexible sound
3. Style
4. Guarantee
   - 100% satisfaction guaranteed!

Step 2 Now, listen to your partner and complete the e-phone conclusion.

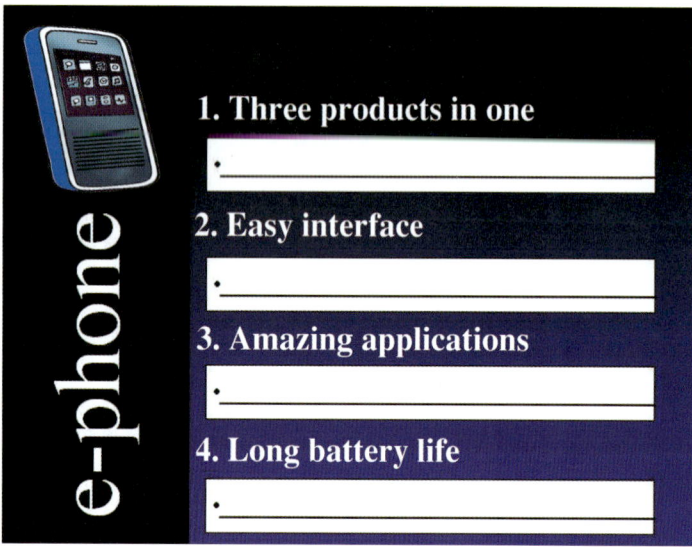

e-phone
1. Three products in one
2. Easy interface
3. Amazing applications
4. Long battery life

Step 3 Use your e-guitar conclusion slide to present your e-guitar conclusion to your partner.

- Overview
    1. Easy to play
    2. Flexible sound
    3. Style
    4. Guarantee
- **1. Easy to Play**
    - Automatic tuning
    - Long, wide neck
    - Light body

    Remember: Always in tune!
- **2. Flexible Sound**
    - Built in synthesizer
    - Master volume control
    - 6-tone settings

    Remember: From mellow acoustic to heavy metal thunder!
- **3. Style**
    - Available in 4 different body shapes
    - Available in 10 different colors

    Remember: Your choice of shape and color!
- **4. Guarantee**
    - No risk, money back guarantee
    - 2-week free trial period

    Remember: 100% satisfaction guaranteed!

Practice: Conclusion

Step 1 Below is a demonstration speech with some steps missing. Write the letter of the picture from the next page in the space provided below.

1	2	3
Hello! I'm Mr. Nicewrench. Today, I'm going to teach you how to change a tire. If you learn this, you won't have to call a garage every time you have a flat tire.		
4	**5** The second step is to block the other three tires with a piece of wood, a rock, or a brick, to keep the car from rolling.	**6** The third and most important point in getting your car ready is to set the jack. You must place the jack under the frame of the car, not under the body or the fender.
7	**8**	**9**
10	**11**	**12**
13 First, set the new tire on the bolts. Put on the lug nuts and tighten them with your fingers.	**14**	**15** Last of all, don't forget to replace the hubcap. Tap it back in place with a rubber hammer or your fist.

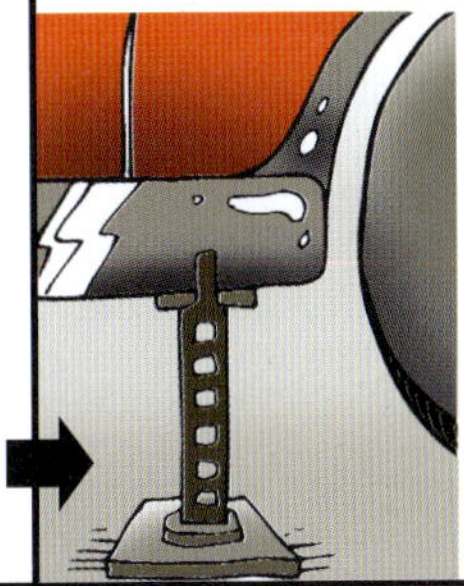

  **Step 2** Now, listen and check your answers.

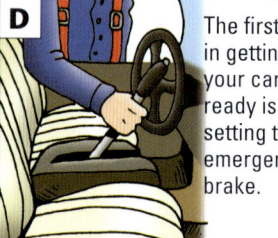

A Last, to get your car ready, move the jack handle up and down to lift the car.

B First, I'll show you how to get the car ready. Second, I'm going to tell you how to take the flat tire off. Last, I'll tell you how to put on the spare tire.

C Next, use the lug wrench to tighten the lug nuts firmly. Turn the nuts clockwise to tighten.

D The first step in getting your car ready is setting the emergency brake.

E We have removed the flat tire. Now, how do we put on the spare tire?

F I have finished explaining how to get your car ready to change the flat tire. Next, I will describe how to remove the flat tire.

G Start by using a flat-blade screwdriver to remove the hubcap.

H Finally, as you remove the lug nuts, place them in the hubcap so they won't get lost. You can now pull off the flat tire.

I Let's look at how to get the car ready to change the tire.

J After that, use a lug wrench to loosen the lug nuts. Remember to turn the wrench counter-clockwise.

Step 3 In the previous speech about how to change a tire, there was no conclusion. In your group, write a conclusion by summarizing the main points from the overview and the phrases stating what to remember for each point.

How to Change a Tire

- **First main point:** ....
  Focus point: ....
- **Second main point:** ....
  Focus point: ....
- **Third main point:** ....
  Focus point: ....

Step 4 Now listen to a sample conclusion.

PERFORMANCE

Conclusion

SPEECH TYPE:

In Episode 8 of the *Speaking of Speech* DVD, three speakers conclude their persuasive presentations. Each conclusion brings together the main points from the body and the focus points from the conclusion. This provides a very simple, clear summary, easily remembered by the audience.

3 CONCLUSION
- Main Point 1
  Focus Point
- Main Point 2
  Focus Point
- Main Point 3
  Focus Point

SPEECH SKILL:

In the conclusion of your persuasive presentation, you will repeat the main points from the overview of your presentation and add focus points from the body of your presentation.

Conclusion

1. Compared: features and benefits

   *Finger grip and pocket clip

2. Demonstrated: special application

   *Guaranteed to work

3. Compared: cost/performance

   *2 pens in 1

SPEECH PREPARATION:

For this presentation, you will prepare a summary chart similar to the ones used by the three speakers in Episode 8 of the DVD.

The Story Message

PERFORMANCE

Model: Conclusion

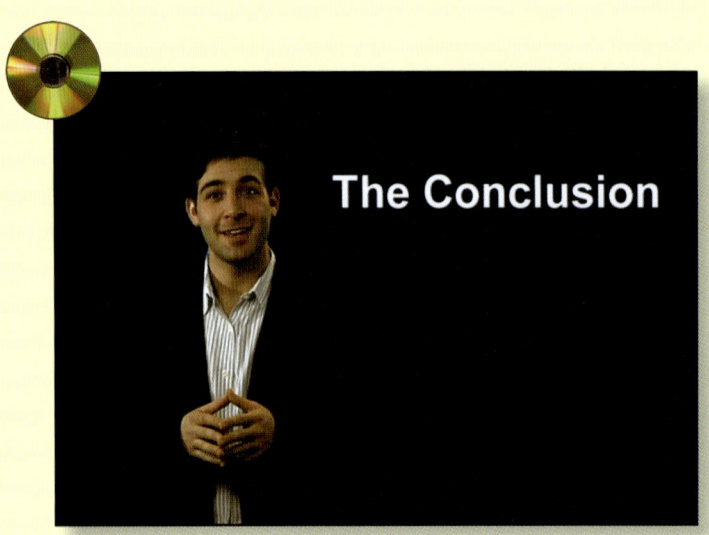

FIRST VIEWING:

Watch Episode 8 of the DVD. Close your textbooks and enjoy the speech! After viewing, answer these questions:

1. What products did the speakers present?
2. Did the speakers follow the same pattern for their conclusions?

SECOND VIEWING:

Watch again and complete the evaluation form below. Fill in the speaker's name, the product, the main points, and the focus points.

Performance Evaluation Form—Conclusion

Speaker's name: / Product:	Main points	Focus points
Speaker's name: / Product:		
Speaker's name: / Product:		
Speaker's name: / Product:		

Speech Preparation

Assignment: Prepare the conclusion of your product presentation.

Step 1 — PLAN:
Copy the main points of your overview chart onto your conclusion chart. Choose focus points that you want the audience to remember and put those on the chart.

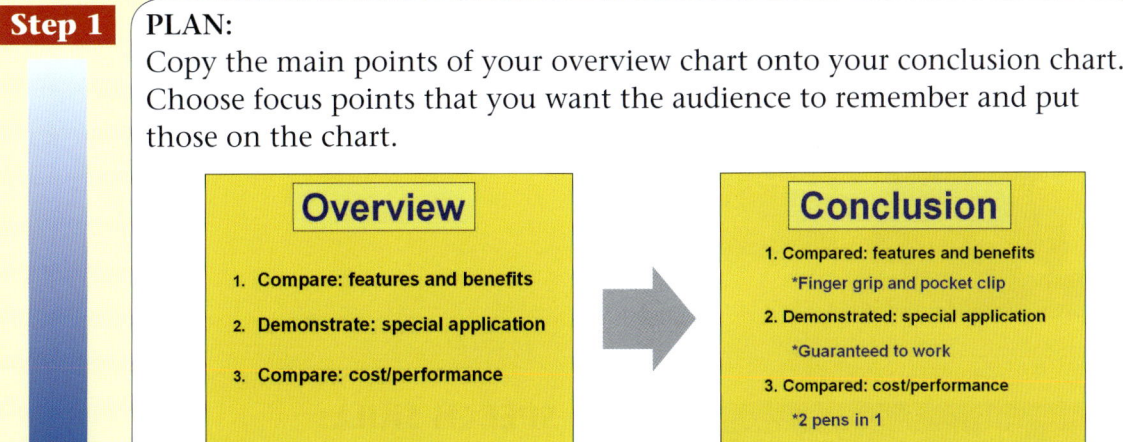

Step 2 — PREPARE:
Make your conclusion chart. You can prepare your chart on a computer and print it out or prepare a poster, or whatever media is appropriate.

Step 3 — PRACTICE:
Focus on making a quick, clear, persuasive conclusion. Point to the information on the chart as you summarize.

Step 4 — PERFORM:
Speakers, present the conclusion of your product presentation. Listeners, fill in the evaluation form on page 106.

FINAL PERFORMANCE

SPEECH TYPE:

In the final performance, you will combine the introduction, the body, and the conclusion into one complete speech.

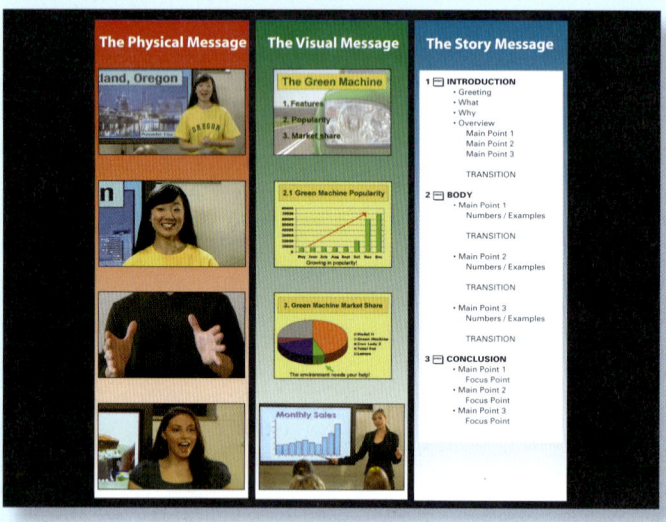

SPEECH SKILL:

The final performance is your opportunity to practice the skills of all three messages. During your presentation, the audience will be evaluating your Physical Message, your Visual Message, and your Story Message.

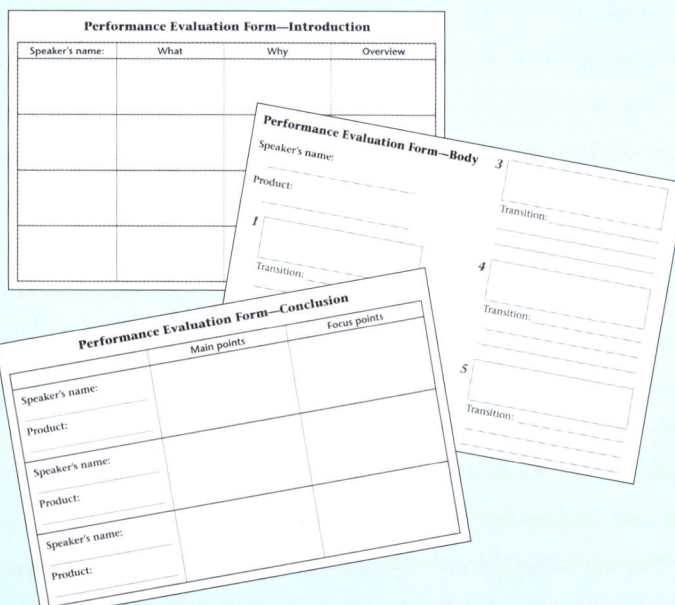

SPEECH PREPARATION:

Review the feedback you received after the performance of your introduction, after the performance of your body, and the after the performance of your conclusion. Use this feedback to improve your final performance.

Speaking of Speech New Edition

In preparation for your final performance, you are going to watch Justin's introduction, body, and conclusion again. While you watch, fill out the form on the next page evaluating his Physical Message, his Visual Message, and his Story Message.

Watch the introduction of Justin's presentation in Episode 6 of the DVD.

Watch the body of Justin's presentation in Episode 7 of the DVD.

Watch the conclusion of Justin's presentation in Episode 8 of the DVD.

FINAL PERFORMANCE

Final Performance Evaluation Sheet

Speaker's name: _Justin Martin_

Physical Message (Circle the appropriate numbers)

	Lowest				Highest
Posture	1	2	3	4	5
Eye Contact	1	2	3	4	5
Gestures	1	2	3	4	5
Voice Inflection	1	2	3	4	5

What did the speaker do that you liked best? _____
_____
_____
_____

Visual Message (Circle the appropriate numbers)

	Lowest				Highest
Quality of Visuals	1	2	3	4	5
Use of Visuals	1	2	3	4	5

Which visual did you like best? _____
_____
_____
_____

Story Message (Circle the appropriate numbers)

	Lowest				Highest
Introduction	1	2	3	4	5
Body and Evidence	1	2	3	4	5
Transitions and Sequencers	1	2	3	4	5
Conclusion	1	2	3	4	5

What was best about the speaker's Story Message? _____
_____
_____
_____

Speaking of Speech New Edition

Speech Preparation

Assignment: Combine the introduction, the body, and the conclusion of your product presentation into one complete presentation.

Step 1 — **PLAN:**
Review the feedback you have gotten from your previous performances. What did you do well? What did you want to improve for your final performance?

Step 2 — **PREPARE:**
Use the table below to evaluate your strong points and weak points.

	Strong points	Weak points
Physical Message		
Visual Message		
Story Message		

If you found that your **Physical Message** needs work, review units 1, 2 and 3 and practice your delivery in the next step. If you found that your **Visual Message** needs improvement, review units 4 and 5 and rework your visuals. If you found that your **Story Message** needs work, review units 6, 7, and 8 and improve your story.

Step 3 — **PRACTICE:**
Deliver your presentation and time it. Is it too long? Is it too short?

Step 4 — **PERFORM:**
Speakers, present your complete presentation. Listeners, use the evaluation form on page 107. When you are finished, use the Final Performance Evaluation Totalizer to calculate your final score. Have fun in your final *Speaking of Speech* performance!

Informative Speech Evaluation Form

Speaker's name: _____ City: _____

SEE	DO
EAT	**GETTING AROUND**

Did the speaker use the Posture & Eye Contact Checklist? ☐ Yes ☐ No

Did the speaker look at you? ☐ Yes ☐ No

Informative Speech Evaluation Form

Speaker's name: _____ City: _____

SEE	DO
EAT	**GETTING AROUND**

Did the speaker use the Posture & Eye Contact Checklist? ☐ Yes ☐ No

Did the speaker look at you? ☐ Yes ☐ No

Layout Speech Evaluation Form

Speaker's name: _____ Place: _____

Did the speaker use gestures? ☐ Yes ☐ No

Layout Speech Evaluation Form

Speaker's name: _____ Place: _____

Did the speaker use gestures? ☐ Yes ☐ No

Demonstration Speech Evaluation Form

Speaker's name: _____

What did the speaker demonstrate?: _____

Steps	Warnings

Did the speaker use voice inflection? ☐ Yes ☐ No

Demonstration Speech Evaluation Form

Speaker's name: _____

What did the speaker demonstrate?: _____

Steps	Warnings

Did the speaker use voice inflection? ☐ Yes ☐ No

Country Comparison Speech Evaluation Form

Speaker's name: _____   Countries: _____

1st point of comparison	2nd point of comparison	3rd point of comparison

Used I.E.E.?   ☐ Yes   ☐ No

Country Comparison Speech Evaluation Form

Speaker's name: _____   Countries: _____

1st point of comparison	2nd point of comparison	3rd point of comparison

Used I.E.E.?   ☐ Yes   ☐ No

Performance Evaluation Form—Introduction

Speaker's name:	What	Why	Overview

Performance Evaluation Form—Introduction

Speaker's name:	What	Why	Overview

Performance Evaluation Form—Body

Speaker's name: _____

Product: _____

1. _____
   Transition: _____

2. _____
   Transition: _____

3. _____
   Transition: _____

4. _____
   Transition: _____

5. _____
   Transition: _____

Performance Evaluation Form—Body

Speaker's name: _____

Product: _____

1. _____
   Transition: _____

2. _____
   Transition: _____

3. _____
   Transition: _____

4. _____
   Transition: _____

5. _____
   Transition: _____

Performance Evaluation Form—Conclusion

	Main points	Focus points
Speaker's name: Product:		
Speaker's name: Product:		
Speaker's name: Product:		

Performance Evaluation Form—Conclusion

	Main points	Focus points
Speaker's name: Product:		
Speaker's name: Product:		
Speaker's name: Product:		

Final Performance Evaluation Sheet

Speaker's name: _____

Physical Message (Circle the appropriate numbers)

	Lowest				Highest
Posture	1	2	3	4	5
Eye Contact	1	2	3	4	5
Gestures	1	2	3	4	5
Voice Inflection	1	2	3	4	5

What did the speaker do that you liked best? _____

_____

_____

Visual Message (Circle the appropriate numbers)

	Lowest				Highest
Quality of Visuals	1	2	3	4	5
Use of Visuals	1	2	3	4	5

Which visual did you like best? _____

_____

_____

Story Message (Circle the appropriate numbers)

	Lowest				Highest
Introduction	1	2	3	4	5
Body and Evidence	1	2	3	4	5
Transitions and Sequencers	1	2	3	4	5
Conclusion	1	2	3	4	5

What was best about the speaker's Story Message? _____

_____

_____

Final Performance Evaluation Totalizer

After your speech, collect the evaluation sheets from the listeners and write the numbers in the spaces provided below. (If you have more than three evaluation sheets, continue on another sheet of paper.) Total up your scores for each column (T) and divide that total by the number of people who gave you an evaluation sheet (P). This is your final score for each of the skill areas covered in *Speaking of Speech*.

Physical Message

	Posture	Eye Contact	Gestures	Voice Inflection
Evaluation 1				
Evaluation 2				
Evaluation 3				
Total of each column (T)	(T1)	(T2)	(T3)	(T4)

Final Score

$$\frac{T1+T2+T3+T4}{P} = \boxed{}$$

Visual Message

	Quality of Visuals	Use of Visuals
Evaluation 1		
Evaluation 2		
Evaluation 3		
Total of each column (T)	(T1)	(T2)

Final Score

$$\frac{T1+T2}{P} = \boxed{}$$

Story Message

	Introduction	Body and Evidence	Transitions and Sequencers	Conclusion
Evaluation 1				
Evaluation 2				
Evaluation 3				
Total of each column (T)	(T1)	(T2)	(T3)	(T4)

Final Score

$$\frac{T1+T2+T3+T4}{P} = \boxed{}$$

How did you do in each skill area?

- **Score between 1 and 2:** You need to go back and read the section on this skill area again. As you read the section try to identify your weak points.
- **Score between 2 and 3:** More improvement is necessary. You will need to work hard in this skill area to become a good public speaker.
- **Score between 3 and 4:** Good. You have a good knowledge of this skill area and with practice you will become a good public speaker.
- **Score between 4 and 5:** Congratulations! You are well on your way to becoming an accomplished public speaker.

About the Authors

David Harrington has been involved in English language teaching for over 20 years. He has taught students of almost every age and circumstance from preschoolers to graduate students. He was the founder of the book distribution companies, The English Resource and Independent Publishers International. David has also co-authored several books including *Discover Debate*, *Getting Ready for Speech*, *Discussion Process* and *Principle, What's in the Cards*, and *Street Speak*. David currently teaches at Ferris Women's University and Showa Women's University and in his spare time, is the managing director of Compass Publishing Japan.

Charles LeBeau was once an aspiring jazz musician a long time ago in a galaxy far, far away. Since landing in Japan in 1982, he has taught in both the university and corporate worlds. Currently, he teaches at two universities and is on the faculty of the Toshiba International Training Center, where he has taught for over 20 years. He divides his time between Yokohama, Japan and Eugene, Oregon, where hippies with VW buses and tie-dyed shirts still flourish.

Authors' Acknowledgments

The legendary UCLA basketball coach, John Wooden, once said it takes 10 hands to score a basket. This is even truer for making a book. The authors would like to thank the following people for their invaluable help and support: First, the late Bill Balsamo, president of Himeiji JALT, founder of Teachers Helping Teachers, and sponsor of charity projects that span the globe, for his humble example that life is about being of service to others. Don Hinkleman for his long and loyal support of SOS, and more recently, development of the SOS Moodle site. Yoko Morimoto, Assistant Professor at Meiji University, for sharing her vision of the new edition with Charles at the "Meet the Stars" session of JALT 2007. Susan Meiki for the explicit handouts showing exactly how she uses the book. Sophia Shang for demonstrating that there is a market for SOS outside Japan. Lorraine Sakka, Associate Professor at Fukui University, for her enthusiastic support of all of our books. Mark Coughlin for his long and loyal use of SOS. Kris Young and Melodie Cook for their enthusiasm and support. At Macmillan UK the authors would like to thank Marc Goozée and Cathren Jones. At Macmillan Japan, Haruo Ono, Alastair Lamond, Euan McKirdy, and Robert Habbick, and last, but not least, Toru Komiya who caught many, many errors and misspellings, and who labored long, long hours to make this book happen.

David Harrington would like to thank:
My wonderful wife, Mami Ushida Harrington, and four beautiful children, Kikiyo Marie Harrington, Tsukasa James Harrington, Tyler Patrick Harrington and Kilan Masami Harrington for teaching me what love has to do with it.

Charles LeBeau would like to thank:
My parents for not giving up on me; my brothers for putting up with me; my sons for inspiring me; and my wife for patiently showing me how to have an adult relationship. Life is good—and I have never had it so good!

MACMILLAN LANGUAGEHOUSE LTD., TOKYO
ISBN: 978-0-2307-2601-7

Macmillan Education
4 Crinan Street
London N1 9XW
A division of Macmillan Publishers Limited
Companies and representatives throughout the world

ISBN: 978-0-2307-1533-2

Text © David Harrington & Charles LeBeau 2009
Design and illustration © Macmillan LanguageHouse Ltd., Tokyo / Macmillan Publishers Limited 2009

First published 1996
This edition 2009

All rights reserved; no part of this publication may be reproduced, stored in a retrieval system, transmitted in any form, or by any means, electronic, mechanical, photocopying, recording, or otherwise, without the prior written permission of the publishers.

Photocopies may be made, for classroom use, of pages 100–108 without the prior written permission of Macmillan Publishers Limited. However, please note that the copyright law, which does not normally permit multiple copying of published material, applies to the rest of this book.

Designed by KYcreates and Language Solutions, Inc.
Illustrated by Ty Semaka and Illustrators MOCO
Illustrations on pages 27 and 72, and photographs on page 110 courtesy of Language Solutions, Inc.
Cover photographs by iStockPhoto and Mannic Media
Cover illustration by Ty Semaka

The authors and publishers would like to thank the following for permission to reproduce their photographic material:
iStockPhoto, Getty Images (pp. 27, 28, 32, 33, 34, 35), PHOTODISC (pp. 27, 32, 34, 48), U.S. Department of Energy's Atmospheric Radiation Measurement Program (pp. 33, 35), Stockbyte (p. 45)
Commissioned photographs by Mannic Media

The publishers would like to thank the following for their assistance in the development of this textbook (in alphabetical order):

William S. Anton
Kyoko Arai
Bram Barker
Paul Batten
Patrick Bencke
Alan Bergman
Anthony Crooks
Peter Dine
Kaduhr Donald
John Dougill
Amanda Gaunt
Patrick Harrington
Neil Heffernan
Tomoyoshi Iwasa
Midori Kanmei
Kathrine Kanno
Keita Kikuchi
Margaret C. Kim
Jonathan S. Kohn
Joe Luckett
Charles McHugh
Sean Mehmet
Kevin Mueller
Masanori Nakamura
Tamah Nakamura
Fumie Noguchi
Kyoko Okamoto
Clark Richardson
Tony Ryan
Lorraine Sakka
Urszula Styczek
Mikiko Sudo
Tomoko Sugihashi
Aya Suzuki
Hiroshi Takubo
Jayna Tanaka
Nicolas Walters
Mark Wright
Kyoko Yamakoshi

Printed and bound in Thailand

2020 2019 2018 2017
19 18 17 16 15 14 13 12